THE MAGIC OF

Meditation

stories and practices to develop
gratitude and empathy with your child

Marie-Christine Champeaux-Cunin &
Dominique Butet

Translated by Sherab Chödzin Kohn
Foreword by Matthieu Ricard

Shambhala
Boulder 2018

Shambhala Publications, Inc.
4720 Walnut Street
Boulder, Colorado 80301
www.shambhala.com

Illustrations by Adejie

This was previously published in French as *La méditation pour les enfants: Une initiation avec Yupsi le petit dragon.*

9 8 7 6 5 4 3 2 1

First U.S. Edition
Printed in the United States of America

⊗ This edition is printed on acid-free paper that meets the American National Standards Institute Z39.48 Standard.
♻ Shambhala makes every effort to print on recyled paper. For more information please visit www.shambhala.com.

Distributed in the United States by Penguin Random House LLC and in Canada by Random House of Canada Ltd

Designed by Liz Quan

Library of Congress Cataloging-in-Publication Data
Names: Champeaux-Cunin, Marie-Christine, author. | Butet, Dominique, author.
  Chödzin, Sherab, translator. | Ricard, Matthieu, writer of introduction.
Title: The magic of meditation: stories and practices to develop gratitude and empathy
  with your child / Marie-Christine Champeaux-Cunin and Dominique Butet; translated
  by Sherab Chödzin Kohn.
Other titles: Méditation pour les enfants | Stories and practices to develop gratitude and
  empathy with your child
Description: Boulder, Colorado: Shambhala Publications, Inc., 2018. | In English,
  translated by the original French. | Includes bibliographical references.
Identifiers: LCCN 2017048142 | ISBN 9781611805291 (pbk.: alk. paper)
Subjects: LCSH: Champeaux-Cunin, Marie-Christine. Méditation pour les enfants. |
  Butet, Dominique. Méditation pour les enfants. | Meditation for children. | Meditation—
  Buddhism—Juvenile literature. | Dragons—Juvenile fiction.
Classification: LCC BF723.M37 C43 2018 | DDC 158.1/2083—dc23
LC record available at https://lccn.loc.gov/2017048142

In homage to
His Eminence Gyalwa Dokhampa
and Jigme Pema Nyinjadh

To Alexandra and to all the children
in the world and their parents

Contents

Foreword by Matthieu Ricard ix

Introduction xiii

PART ONE: Introduction to Meditation **1**

1. What Is Meditation? 3
2. Why Meditate? 8
3. Which Meditation Practice to Choose? 19

PART TWO: Meditation for Your Child **31**

4. Meditation Starting at Age Three 33
5. The Benefits of Meditation for Your Child 36
6. Introduction to the Yupsi Method 43

PART THREE: The Yupsi Stories and Meditations **55**

7. The Gift Stickers Test: Your Child's Initial Level of
  Compassion 57

Contents

8. Every Evening, Do What Yupsi Does   59
  The Lotus (or Cross-Legged) Position   59
  Three-Breath Meditation   60
  Meditation on Appreciation   61
  Dedication to All the Children in the World   61

9. The Yupsi Stories   62
  The Blue Donkey Who Rode a Bike   62
  The Butterfly Kite   65
  Trouble in the Land of the Bees   68
  The Snowshoe Hare Caught in a Frozen Waterfall   72
  The Child from Ladakh   76
  The Child with the Bandage   79
  The Wild Kittens   83
  The Via Ferrata of Joy   87

10. Meditations for Older Kids, Starting at Age Five   92
  Meditation on the Breath: White Light and
   Black Smoke   93
  Meditation on Appreciation   95
  Dedication to All the Children in the World   96
  Walking Meditation   96

11. The Gift Stickers Test: Your Child's Level of
  Compassion after Ten Weeks of the Program   99

Conclusion   101
Acknowledgments   103
Notes   105

Foreword

The idea of introducing periods of meditation into the school curricu-
lum generally arouses uneasiness and apprehension in both parents
and teachers. But if you offer these same people a secular program
based on reliable scientific studies that improves attention, emotional
balance, and personal relations among students, they welcome it with
open arms. Programs based on meditation, or—to use a less culturally
loaded expression—mind training, have been in place in England, the
Netherlands, the United States, Canada, Australia, and a number of other
countries for quite a few years now, to the benefit of a large number of
students.

A growing number of children are suffering from problems with
attention, emotional disorders, and relationship difficulties, and the
average age of the first appearance of depression has gone down from
twenty-seven to fifteen over the last twenty-five years. In this challen-
ging environment, meditation offers a way to strengthen the psychological immune system in the same way physical exercise strengthens
the physical immune system.

In school we teach children a variety of disciplines, how to pass a test, and how to succeed. All important, no doubt, but if we ask parents what they want the most for their children, most of them will reply with words such as happiness, self-confidence, joy, kindness, health, love, and a meaningful life. Beyond reading, writing, and arithmetic, schools have the opportunity to teach children how to become better human beings.

Marie-Christine Champeaux-Cumin and Dominique Butet's *Magic of Meditation* provides a welcome introduction to meditation to both parents and children. The authors clearly explain what meditation is (a way of training the mind) and what it is not (a mere exercise in relaxation and a vain attempt to empty the mind). The first two parts of the book explain what meditation is for parents and children; the third part illustrates the practice of meditation in the form of stories for children.

It is important for us to understand that the goal of meditation is not to impose an artificial way of thinking on children; instead, the practice helps them to bring out the best in themselves, fostering their natural inclination toward cooperation and altruism.

Very early in life, even as babies, we show a preference for people who behave kindly toward others over people who treat others with hostility. At Yale University, Paul Bloom's researchers showed a video to children between the ages of six and ten months in which a ball with large eyes is having trouble getting up a steep incline. A second ball enters the scene and helps the first one by pushing it from behind. Then a third ball comes along and gives the first ball a downward push, causing it to tumble all the way back down to the bottom of the incline. The babies were then offered two balls, one resembling the second and one resembling the third. Nine out of ten of the babies reached out toward the second ball, the one that had been kind and helpful.

In Vancouver, a group of psychologists demonstrated that two-year-old children were happier when they gave a treat to somebody else than when they received one.

At the Max Planck Institute in Leipzig, Michael Tomasello and Felix Warneken established that children at the age of one, at a time when they are still barely learning to walk and talk, already demonstrate behaviors of mutual aid and cooperation without having learned them from an adult. And being rewarded didn't necessarily serve as motivation; in fact, those who were rewarded were less helpful than those who received nothing.

Programs for cultivating attention and kindness by means of meditation have already demonstrated their value. Examples include the compassion training introduced at the preschool level in Madison, Wisconsin, by the team of neuroscientist Richard Davidson and the program of cognitive therapy based on compassion for children living in foster homes founded by psychiatrist Chuck Raison at Emory University in Atlanta, Georgia. We can also point to Neil Hawkes's values-based education program in England and programs for the development of emotional intelligence in place in hundreds of schools throughout the world.

Education is an opportunity to nurture and strengthen children's natural inclination toward empathy and altruism. An enlightened education emphasizes the interdependence that exists among human beings, animals, and our natural environment and encourages children to choose cooperation over competition and active concern over indifference. In this way, children can grow up with a holistic view of the world that surrounds them and naturally make positive contributions to their communities.

I am quite confident that reading about the magic breath of Yupsi the Little Dragon and learning to practically apply the lessons contained in the stories will provide precious tools for an education that, to paraphrase Aristophanes, does not consist only of filling the vase but also in lighting a flame in it. The flame here is the joy of living and learning—for our own good and for that of society.

—MATTHIEU RICARD

Introduction

Being a parent in the twenty-first century certainly can be a challenge! The world around us is changing so fast that sometimes we feel it is leaving us behind, and the subject of education can be a confusing one. We want education to bring our children happiness and success, and we also want education to prepare them for society's lightning-speed changes and the stress that these changes can bring on. Dealing with the speed of change is one of the great challenges of our time.

New research has shown that the introduction of meditation, starting at the preschool level, has a profound effect on the education of our children. Our book about Yupsi the Little Dragon is inspired by this research and presents a method for practicing meditation with your young child starting as early as the age of three.

You don't have to be somebody who frequents a yoga studio, martial arts dojo, or meditation hall to give this adventure a try. The practices selected for this book are all entirely secular in nature and can be used independently of any philosophical or religious belief.

In part 1, you will find a brief, simple introduction to meditation that will give you an understanding of the basics and benefits of the practice. In part 2, we will talk about the benefits of meditation for your child in terms of health, managing emotions, and success in school. In part 3, we will introduce you and your child to Yupsi the Little Dragon. The stories will compassionately guide your child through the dragon's magic breath to help find calm and work through difficult emotions. Yupsi will help your child find an inner sense of security that will accompany her, like Yupsi, all through her life.

Introducing your child to meditation is like planting a seed for the future. What sprouts up will of course depend on her personality but also on how you share these special moments with her. We believe that with consistency and perseverance every child is capable of "getting it." It will then fall to you to observe the results and to decide whether the experiment is worth continuing with or not.

This book comes with an audio component that includes the "Yupsi Song" as well as recordings of the meditations and stories. The audio is available for download at www.shambhala.com/magicofmeditation.

Giving your child the opportunity to meditate from a very early age and to practice with him is one of the most wonderful gifts you can give him. We wish you wonderful adventures with your child in the company of Yupsi the Little Dragon and his magic breath.

PART ONE

INTRODUCTION

TO MEDITATION

In today's busy and agitated world, many parents have heard about meditation, but few are actually well informed about the positive effects it can have on their children. In this part of the book, we will define meditation and elaborate on its many benefits. Then we will provide basic instructions on teaching your children how to meditate, give tips on guiding them through this new experience, and share four basic meditative practices.

1 What Is Meditation?

The meaning of the word *meditation* can be different depending on the context. Are we talking about the East or the West? About simply achieving well-being or a spiritual quest?

Two friends were having lunch together. One asked the other, "So, you meditate?"

The other replied, "Sure, I just signed up for a course. And you, have you finally started?"

"Oh, yes," replied the first, "I started a while ago. It's doing me a tremendous amount of good."

Now, if we looked a little deeper, we would find that these two friends weren't actually talking about the same thing. One of them was taking a yoga class and the other was practicing relaxation techniques from an app she just downloaded. In reality, neither one of them had begun to practice meditation.

Another view is that meditation is all about sitting on a cushion and emptying your head of thoughts. But in actuality, the flow of thoughts cannot be controlled easily. In the pages that follow, we'll look at the complex and varied ways meditation can be used so that you can best guide your child as she begins to practice.

The Eastern Origins of Meditation

We find the first written evidence of meditation in the ancient Indian texts called the Vedas, dating back to about 1400 B.C.E. Some scholars believe that meditation was being practiced well before that. In the Vedas, meditation took the form of mantras, Sanskrit formulas that were to be repeated over and over again. The word *mantra* in Sanskrit means "mind-protecting." Mantra recitation was an integral part of yoga, which comes from the Sanskrit word *jug*, which means "to bind, unite": uniting the body, heart, and mind.

In the first millennium B.C.E., Brahmanism and Jainism influenced the practice of meditation in India, and in the sixth century B.C.E., meditation became a fundamental part of Taoism in China and Buddhism in India.

In Buddhism, we learn that *meditation* comes from the Sanskrit term *bhavana*, which means "take care of, cultivate," and from the Tibetan term *gom*, which means "familiarize oneself with." Meditation serves to cultivate the mind by revealing its hidden qualities. Matthieu Ricard defines meditation as "a tool that serves to make us better people and put our good qualities at the service of others. It is a practice that allows us to actualize the potential that lies within us. It is a training of the mind that brings about alertness, kindness, and compassion. It is a path that leads to inner freedom and knowledge of the ultimate reality of things."

This means a Buddhist person seeks to acquire true knowledge of herself and of the functioning of her mind. Through the practice of meditation, she becomes aware of her inner potential and pays close attention to her own behavior and that of those around her.

Meditation is a long-term, progressive effort with a new state of mind gradually settling in. The ultimate goal of meditation is to help ourselves and others to become liberated from the causes of suffering and to achieve true happiness. In Buddhism, it is thought that those who bring genuine love, kindness, and understanding to people around them will receive the direct benefits of their actions in this life or the next.

The Many Meditative Paths of the West

While most Westerners immediately associate meditation with Eastern religions, it was also used by ancient Greek philosophers and Christians in the Middle Ages as a contemplative practice. The word *meditation* comes from the Greek word *melete*, which means "training" or "exercise." It was transcribed in Latin as *meditatio*, which means more or less "to pay attention to an object of thought."

From the beginning of the fifth century B.C.E., meditation occupied a key spot in philosophical debate. Socrates, who is considered the father of Western philosophy, focused his attention on the nature of being human. He inquired into the knowledge of self, the nature of truth and beauty, and the notions of good, immortality, and the soul. To Socrates, being a philosopher meant being able to withdraw into the deepest level of oneself, principally by means of meditation. Socrates was followed by Aristotle, founder of the Peripatetic school of the Lyceum, situated on a walkway (*peripatos*), where the master taught as he walked back and forth. In his *Nicomachean Ethics*, Aristotle distinguished three types of happiness: pleasure, politics, and meditation. Only the last of these found favor in his eyes, because "only the contemplative life can bring contentment to the wise man and permit him to live according to reason and in harmony with the nature of man and that of the universe." A half-century later, the philosopher Epicurus proposed another more therapeutic kind of meditation using techniques for overcoming pain.

Among the founding fathers of the Church, the theologians who established Christian doctrine following the Apostles were mainly concerned with unifying the body, soul, and mind. This kind of reflection enabled the Eastern Christian tradition to develop powerful tools of concentration and relaxation. The Prayer of the Heart, or *hesychasm* (which comes from the Greek *hesuchia*, meaning "tranquility" or "silence"), is still practiced today by the monks of Mount Athos, and this practice represents the fundamental spiritual path of the Greek Orthodox Church.

In the Roman Church, it is silent prayer, in which the faithful attempt to create silence in themselves in order to open themselves to God, that is the principal method. In the sixteenth century, St. Ignatius Loyola, founder of the Society of Jesus, offered "spiritual exercises" in his book of the same name that are still in use today.

In Judaism, Ecstatic Kabbalah and other branches emphasize meditation based on the letters of the Torah and the seventy-two names of God. Sufi meditation draws its inspiration from the Quran; it encourages introspection, and its contemplative practices involve intensive invocation of the names of Allah.

Meditation in the West Today

A current of secular meditation has been steadily gaining force over the past few decades. Meditation is now recommended by psychotherapists and is unreservedly associated with therapeutic benefits.

In the 1980s, Jon Kabat-Zinn, a professor of medicine, introduced a program called Mindfulness-Based Stress Reduction (MBSR), or "mindfulness" for short. Kabat-Zinn's program integrated therapeutic techniques from meditation for the purpose of dealing with stress, anxiety, and illness. The first clinic for stress reduction was founded at the University of Massachusetts Medical School, where the medically oriented Center for Mindfulness also was started. Today, more than five thousand doctors across the world rely on Kabat-Zinn's work in their practices.

Modern-day mindfulness programs are situated at the crossroads between two seemingly opposing worlds. On one side there is the Eastern philosophical tradition with its Buddhist meditation practices, and on the other side the world of Western scientific research in the fields of psychology and neuroscience.

The exercises used in secular mindfulness programs are derived from the mind-training disciplines of Tibetan Buddhism, but the objectives are rather different. The goal of mindfulness is a therapeutic one: in general, to make the body feel better or find relief from emotional problems. This practice is focused around ourselves. In fact, we often speak of it in terms of "personal development," making this approach somewhat limited. By contrast, the primary motivation of Buddhist meditation is to transform oneself in order to become capable of altruistic love and feel compassion for others.

2 Why Meditate?

Many of us are unsatisfied with our lives. Our daily existence is filled with activities, but they aren't what we need to really feel happy. When by chance we experience moments of inner peace, we find that they pass all too quickly. Our worries are soon gnawing at us again. We might think that endless worrying is inevitable and that it is impossible to change this state of affairs in any way. Our sense of inescapable discontent causes suffering, and we might even take our pain out on other people.

It is possible to remedy this kind of suffering by training our minds. For lasting benefits, a regular, daily meditation practice is essential. What benefits might we expect?

Creating Space around Our Thoughts

When you first start to meditate, even after practicing for several days, the beneficial effects might be hard to see. But don't be discouraged. It is easier to see the results of athletic training after just a few sessions: a runner can see them by looking at his chronometer; the figure skater will successfully complete her triple leap. In meditation—which is also training, but of the mind—the effects are less tangible, but the mechanism is still the same. You need to have a basic minimum of interest in and enthusiasm for the exercise—in this case being mindful and willing to make the efforts necessary to get to the goal. The limitations of the mind are no different from those of the body.

Depending on how regular you are with the practice, your way of seeing things will change, and your mind will become more peaceful and less prone to confusion. You will create a distance between yourself and the daily situations you face—whether they are pleasant, annoying, or even very difficult. Meditation will not prevent you from acting; rather, you will act in a calmer, more controlled, and mindful way.

Meditation allows you to develop inner space so you can pause before reacting, a saving grace that can increase your confidence. You will no longer fear situations getting out of control and carrying you away; you will have the crucial time needed to find the right words to respond. For example, disciplining a child will include firmness, but also love rather than impatience and exasperation. And at work, a small moment of reflection can save you many an impulsive blunder.

Learning to Observe

Each time you finish with an exercise in mind training, get into the habit of observing the effects it has had on your mind. How are you feeling? Are you calmer? Little by little, you will start to experience encouraging shifts.

Taming Disturbing Emotions

Meditation vs. Relaxation

It's a beautiful, sunny afternoon, and we're in a meditation workshop. Our goal is to attain mental calm. Everyone is at work concentrating on

Some Benefits of a More Spacious Mind

By developing a regular practice, you can become more:

- Creative
- Productive
- Attentive to others
- Patient
- Tolerant
- In the here and now
- Confident
- Relaxed and balanced
- Able to observe your thoughts and emotions

the coming and going of the breath. Bellies are swelling, and the breath is rising to the head. Distracting thoughts are coming up, but they aren't being grasped; there's no way anyone is going to launch into an extensive inner dialogue. The thoughts are like fish—they jump out of the river, but they fall right back in. Everyone exhales gently and bellies fall. The exercise lasts half an hour. There's a feeling of tranquility, and some people experience a kind of joy. Peace prevails in the large hall. At the end, one of the participants heaves a huge sigh of satisfaction and says, "Wow, that was really terrific! That forest air is so fresh. That deep breathing completely aerated my brain. I feel totally relaxed!"

But if this participant thinks he has been meditating, he has gotten relaxation and meditation mixed up. Deep relaxation brings a feeling of well-being in the moment. Practiced regularly, it can even bring a sense of self-improvement. It lessens the worst effects of negative emotions, protects our health, and makes suffering easier to bear. But meditation takes us further. The goal of meditation is to bring out our potential and transform us into kinder people with more concern for others. Without a doubt this requires regular practice over a long period of time, but ultimately meditation enables us to tame our negative emotions.

Finding Proof from Neuroscience

The physical configuration of the brain is not rigidly fixed. Scientific research in the field of neuroplasticity has confirmed that the mind training effects of meditation can shift the wiring of our brains. This means that it is entirely possible to change our way of seeing things. We have a choice: Should we continue to live the way we do today, or should we try to transform ourselves? It is up to each of us to decide.

A study by Richard Davidson at the University of Wisconsin at Madison published in 2004 demonstrates the effect of meditation on the management of destructive emotions. The meditators tested in this first study, all from the Tibetan Buddhist tradition, had each meditated a total of between ten thousand and fifty thousand hours. As the subjects were meditating on compassion, a remarkable increase in rapid oscillations in the gamma frequencies was observed, "of a magnitude never before recorded in the literature of the neurosciences," wrote Davidson. "This seems to show clearly that the brain can be trained and physically modified in a way that few people could have imagined." Studies of this sort have enabled us to discover—or, I should say, rediscover—how much the millennia-old practice of meditation can help us face the challenges of our own times.

An emerging discipline known as social neuroscience has shown that our relationships with others have an unexpected significance. Daniel Goleman, in his book *Social Intelligence*, stresses that wise action entails a "more expanded view [that] leads us to consider within the scope of social intelligence capacities that enrich personal relationships, like empathy and concern." The implications of these discoveries "compel us to re-evaluate how we live our lives."[1] We could best respond to Goleman's call by practicing meditation for opening the heart, compassion, tolerance, and altruism in our lives.

Working with Anger

An overworked woman forgot to pick up her husband's suit at the cleaner, which she promised she would take care of. That evening, anger exploded in the house. The husband was furious. He was due to leave for a conference in a foreign city—and he needed this suit. His plane was leaving first thing in the morning. His wife came back at him with all barrels blazing. She was thoroughly provoked and got right into his anger. Voices got louder and harsh words were said, becoming increasingly violent, completely beyond reason.

Words can have an irreversible effect on our relationships. As Daniel Goleman put it: "When someone dumps their toxic feelings on us—explodes in anger or threats, shows disgust or contempt—they activate in us circuitry for those very same distressing emotions. Their act has potent neurological consequences: emotions are contagious. We 'catch' strong emotions much as we do a rhinovirus—and so can come down with the emotional equivalent of a cold." [2]

Rather than responding to the other person in an uncontrolled, immediate way, why not try to practice compassion and tolerance? Let's make use of the inner space that our meditation practice has opened up for us. It is impossible for us to control the other person, but we *can* control our own reactions. We can take the time to contemplate our own anger in order to put out the fire of the argument and not let ourselves get carried away. We could evoke feelings of tolerance and allow that the other person might also have had a hard day. We will have a better chance to curb our anger if we do the meditations we've shared in the next chapter for a few minutes every day.

At this point in the book, some of you might be thinking: "Is that it? That's just plain common sense. It's obvious." But in reality, there is a huge gap between theory and practice. As the psychoanalyst Nicole Fabre often says, "You don't become a good cook just by reading a cookbook, and you don't get to be a psychoanalyst just by reading all the books on psychoanalysis!" Only by going through diligent, practical mind training can we really learn to behave in a compassionate and tolerant way.

Managing Jealousy

Jealousy is one of the most difficult emotional reactions. No one wants to experience it, as it dooms us to chronic discontent and suffering.

The remedies for jealousy below might seem simplistic, but they are extremely effective.

- When we meet someone more fortunate, don't be jealous. Rather, be happy for him.
- When someone does something good, rejoice rather than be critical.
- When someone is happy, rejoice again. If she is successful, so much the better.

Putting this into practice may be difficult, but with a little mind training, it is completely possible. Giving up the desire to be better than everybody else is a good place to start.

Dealing with Stress and Anxiety

Hans Selye, who completed his medical studies at the University of Montreal in the 1920s, was the first to use the word *stress* in its current application. Selye noticed that all his patients, no matter what their ailments were, had one thing in common: they all gave the impression of being sick. As Selye saw it, they all were suffering from physical stress resulting from their illness. He determined that stress is the reaction of an organism that feels threatened. In small doses, it can be beneficial and provide the energy needed to deal with the challenges of daily life. But if stress is always there, it can have long-term negative health effects.

Stress can be found everywhere: at work, at home, in a marriage, or in the aftermath of a traumatic event. In times of stress, everything goes wrong. We are at a loss as to how to get out of it, and as a result anxiety begins to take over.

To detect stress in advance, keep an eye out for these warning signs:

- You constantly feel overwhelmed.
- You consistently react negatively to situations.
- You overreact to the causes of stress.

The best way to calm our stressed-out minds is to do twenty minutes of meditation every day, preferably working with the breath (see the meditations proposed in the next chapter). When you are suffering from stress, you may not particularly feel like meditating, and a little extra willpower may be in order. As with many things in life, you can't expect it to feel perfect right from the start!

The best way to combat stress is to take action to prevent its effects before it happens, so the work ideally should begin when everything is going well. That way you will be better prepared when a stress-inducing situation comes along. The Meditation on Appreciation page 61 for the little ones; page 95 for the older ones) is extremely useful for training the mind. The more regularly you practice them, the easier it will be to deal with stress.

Recent studies have shown the benefits meditation can have on older people who are suffering from the stresses of loneliness, which can contribute to cardiovascular problems and even Alzheimer's disease. While meditation certainly isn't a cure-all for the issues of the elderly, it does have the capacity to provide comfort.

In Brief

- The antidote to anger is to practice compassion and tolerance.

- The antidote to jealousy is to practice rejoicing in the happiness of others.

- To prevent and manage stress, practice the Meditation on Appreciation (page 61 for the little ones; page 95 for the older ones). Twenty minutes of meditation a day and a daily breathing exercise can also be helpful.

Strengthening Your Health

Managing your emotions can affect your health on three levels: by preventing illness, fighting illness if it has already shown up, and helping with recuperation. Studies have shown that in the two hours after having a major bout of anger, a person is five times more likely to have a heart attack and three times more likely to suffer from a stroke. The inability to deal with stress causes our immune-system defenses to be weakened, resulting in inflammation and, on the cellular level,

Some of the Health Benefits of Meditation

- Cardiovascular protection
- Immune system protection
- Protection against cellular aging
- Support during cancer treatment and recuperation

- Pain management
- Treatment of the symptoms of addiction and depression
- Management of attention-deficit/hyperactivity disorder
- Weight management

According to Christophe André, positive emotions can rebalance our parasympathetic nervous system and slow down cellular aging, thus supporting longevity.

accelerated deterioration of chromosomes. John T. Cacioppo, the director of the Center for Cognitive and Social Neuroscience at the University of Chicago, speaks of surges of stress hormones so violent that they damage genes governing the cells of the immune system.

A group from the University of California at Davis has shown that three months of intensive meditation stimulates the activity of telomerases, enzymes essential for the protection of cells from aging. During meditation, we generate endorphins in the same way we do during athletic activity, thereby providing positive support for our state of mind. In other words, training the mind helps us take care of the body.

There is plenty of proof of the connection of meditation and health. Between 1970 and 2012, the number of scientific studies on the effects of Buddhist-inspired meditation went from ten per year to practically five hundred, according to data cited in an article by Jon Kabat-Zinn in *Change Yourself, Change the World.*[3] The results of these studies are particularly significant for the treatment of depression, addiction, and attention deficit disorder, and also pain management.

Being More Productive at Work

In the past few years, mindfulness practices have made their way into the business world. Every day, companies, like Google and Sodexo, embark on the adventure of meditation, with employees and bosses alike practicing mindfulness for a few minutes a day.

Will meditation become a commercial commodity? A company might launch a meditation program to make employees more efficient and productive in their jobs, but there are other benefits too. Better-managed emotions means better communication between employees and with the boss, and conflicts are more easily defused. These types of shifts can make for a better work atmosphere, one that's based on trust and confidence (with anxiety and work stress reduced all around). It is an experiment well worth trying!

Take a break while you are sitting at your desk for five or ten minutes every day. Concentrate on your breath. Come into the present moment. Follow the movement of your belly as it rises and falls with your breath and your mind becomes calm. Bring your thoughts toward lovingkindness. Matthieu Ricard suggests saying to yourself: "May everyone I am looking at now be happy."

The Benefits of Meditation at Work

- Makes us more efficient
- Enables us to concentrate better
- Fosters creativity
- Strengthens self-confidence
- Improves personal relationships
- Helps avoid burnout
- Helps us feel good about our work

Everyone can benefit from these types of pauses at work, but a more complete practice at home will help us get the most out of them.

Working toward a More Altruistic Society

The meditation programs we see today are typically based on the basic techniques of mind training in Tibetan Buddhism. But at the same time, it is a form of meditation that has neither an ethical nor a spiritual component.

Some experts are sounding alarms about this contemporary turn of events. "A tradition provides an ethical path as well as a path for transcending the self," Dominique Steiner, an expert in stress management, points out. "If everybody comes up with their own recipe, the risk is that many people will end up practicing with the goal of achieving power over themselves and other people." The best way to avoid this outcome is to be sure to include an altruistic motivation in your practice, which we will discuss in the next chapter. These practices will bear fruit not only for ourselves, our children, and our family, but also for the future of our society. Daniel Goleman goes so far as to say that "the crucial challenge for this century will be to expand the circle of those we count among Us, and shrink the numbers we count as Them."[4]

Which Meditation Practice to Choose?

Tibetan Buddhism offers hundreds of meditation practices. It is up to you to choose which ones work best for you. Are you looking solely for the therapeutic aspects of meditation? Would you like to include an altruistic, compassionate motivation? Or are you interested in immersing yourself in the full spiritual path of this tradition?

Remember that the meditation techniques shared here are not based on religion. But they can—if you wish—become the starting point for a journey that goes well beyond simple self-development. If you are moved to pursue a spiritual path, such as Buddhism or Hinduism, we recommend that this be done under the tutelage of an authentic spiritual guide, a person who can serve as an inexhaustible source of inspiration.

We've drawn the meditative exercises in this book from *Why Meditate?* by Matthieu Ricard[1] and *The Restful Mind* by His Eminence Gyalwa Dokhampa, a young master of Tibetan Buddhism who is quite familiar with the ways of the contemporary world.[2]

How to Begin

Now that you have learned a bit about meditation and its benefits, it's time to get started! Meditation is not something you do by reading—it's something you have to practice.

In this chapter, we will offer suggestions that you can use in your everyday life. We will get you acquainted with four important meditation exercises selected from the books mentioned above. As a parent who is looking to introduce moments of meditation into your child's life, it is important for you to prepare yourself by not only reading the exercises but doing them at least once or twice before sharing them with your child.

These same exercises will reappear in part 2, but in a highly simplified form adapted for young children. With your support, as your child gets older and has gathered more experience with meditation, you can start to introduce the more advanced exercises from this chapter.

When you see how thrilled your child is to share this new activity with you, your efforts will be rewarded. What is good for you is also good for your child. Little by little, both you and your child will notice the benefits of a meditation practice.

There are several ways of practicing meditation in our busy lives. A short, regular, daily meditation is more valuable than an occasional long session. A few minutes a day isn't enough to bring about a real transformation, but it's enough to begin with.

You might believe that your mind is so restless that you won't be able to sit still on a cushion without getting impatient. Your mind is filled with a long list of things you have to do, all of them of the very highest importance (water the plants, update social media, answer phone messages, and so on). But the first order of business should be to pacify your mind, which is why morning might be the best time to meditate.

The simplest technique for taming the ceaseless whirling of thoughts in our minds is to do what comes most naturally: inhale and exhale. By meditating on the breath, your ability to concentrate will gradually increase, and eventually you'll be able to keep it up for twenty minutes, which is the recommended practice time for a beginner. In addition to a formal practice, try getting into the habit of performing your daily tasks mindfully. This means heightening your perceptions while remaining fully relaxed in the present moment. Washing dishes or emptying the dishwasher can be quite calming if you do them with full attention.

When you are caught in a traffic jam, it is useless to keep changing lanes and getting yourself worked up by trying to get a few cars ahead— the reality is, it's hopeless! On the other hand, what *is* within your control is the way you react to the situation. By meditating on the in-breath and out-breath, you will learn to give yourself a little space and accept the fact that everything might not always go the way you planned it.

EXERCISE

Meditation on the Coming and Going of the Breath (based on the description by Matthieu Ricard)

1. Sit in a comfortable position, with your body upright and well balanced. Here, mindfulness means remaining aware of your breathing without forgetting it or letting yourself be distracted.

2. Breathe calmly and naturally. Concentrate all your attention on the coming and going of the breath. More specifically, focus

your attention on the sensation created by the passage of air through your nostrils. Also notice the moment when breathing is suspended—between the out-breath and the following in-breath. After that, concentrate again on the point where you feel the breath passing. Then, note the moment when the breath pauses between the in-breath and the out-breath.

3. Continue another cycle of breathing, breath after breath, without tensing up and without relaxing to the point of becoming sluggish. Let your awareness of the breath be clear and calm.

4. Do not intentionally change the rhythm of your breath. Your breathing will probably slow a little; allow it to happen naturally. Whether your breath is long or short, simply be aware of the fact that it is long or short.

5. Sooner or later, you will wander into a state of distraction accompanied by many thoughts or into a slightly sleepy state. Or you might even experience a combination of both—a state of confusion marked by erratic thought associations. Be vigilant; as soon as you notice you have lost your concentration, simply return to the breath without adding feelings of regret or guilt to your distraction. Noticing the distraction already marks the return of your mindfulness. Just come back to the breath, like a butterfly coming back to a flower after having fluttered around here and there for no apparent reason.

6. When thoughts appear, don't try to block them (which isn't possible, because they are already there); just avoid feeding them. Let them pass through the field of your awareness the way a bird passes through the sky without leaving a trace.

Another good habit to get into is taking micro-pauses in the course of a busy day. Feeling like you never have any extra time is the sign of an agitated mind. If you are experiencing upsetting emotions, short pauses following the breath can help. Take time out for a brief meditation with the phone turned off. Say to yourself, "Watch your breath. Breathe gently for a few minutes."

Finding the Time to Meditate

As we mentioned earlier, the same discipline that you apply in athletic training—or for finger exercises if you are a musician—is required in mind training. In all cases, the efforts you make toward acquiring a sense of well-being and balance in your life are well worth it. A few minutes a day is all it takes, and you won't regret having taken them!

Patience and Perseverance

When you begin your meditation practice, your mind will be full of distractions, and it won't be easy to get it to settle down. Sometimes it will remain agitated for the entire practice. Other obstacles will appear—the phone will ring, the baby will wake up and cry, or your older child will walk in and ask for help with his homework, to say nothing of the pain in your knees!

There are a number of ways you might react to these common obstacles. One would be to get irritated and jump to the conclusion that you've failed and have been wasting your time. Another possibility is to change your perspective and look at the obstacles as integral to your experience and stepping-stones in your progress. At the beginning you will need to arm yourself with patience and perseverance, as you would with any new activity.

Meditation on the Breath with Visualization

Here is another meditation based on the breath that has been recommended by His Eminence Gyalwa Dokhampa. Meditations and breathing exercises involving specific physical postures are valuable for engaging the body in calming the mind. This practice, which looks like a yoga exercise, is excellent for maintaining health. You can also engage the seven-point posture while doing the Meditation on the Coming and Going of the Breath (page 21).

EXERCISE

The Seven-Point Posture

1. Cross-legged (or in lotus or half-lotus), left leg inside

2. Straight back, like a stack of coins

3. Shoulders stretched straight, like the wings of an eagle

4. Neck slightly bent forward

5. Eyes open, focused, with gaze lowered, to about three feet in front of you

6. Mouth slightly open with the tip of the tongue touching the upper palate

7. Hands on lap, right palm over left, with thumbs touching[3]

If you have knee problems, you may sit on a low bench or a chair with your back straight and not resting against the back of the chair. Keep your feet parallel and flat on the floor.

In the following meditation, you will be asked to visualize the positive aspects of the world, imagining that they enter you on the in-breath in the form of white light. Then on the exhale, you will visualize all that's negative inside you—anger, jealousy, sadness—imagining that they come out of you in the form of black smoke.

Beginners can repeat the exercise three times, with each repetition starting at the second step. As your practice grows, you can increase the number of repetitions.

EXERCISE

Meditation on the Breath: White Light and Black Smoke

1. Begin with a long exhalation through both nostrils and visualize anger, hatred, negative karma, disappointment, and stress coming out of you in the form of black smoke.

2. Close your left nostril with your finger and inhale deeply through your right nostril. Hold the breath for two seconds and visualize all that's positive going into your body in the form of white light.

3. Close your right nostril and exhale negative thoughts through your left nostril in the form of black smoke.

4. Inhale one more time through your left nostril while visualizing positive thoughts in the form of white light.

5. Close your left nostril and exhale negative thoughts through your right nostril in the form of black smoke.

6. Inhale deeply through both nostrils while visualizing positive thoughts in the form of white light.

7. Forcefully exhale negative thoughts through both nostrils in the form of black smoke.

Benefits

When you practice this meditation on the breath, you simply bring your mind back to the present moment, without desire or expectation. You put your mind at rest. By practicing it every day, you'll find that the feeling of calm it brings lasts longer and longer.

Meditation on the breath is not only calming, it is also stimulating, and over time it becomes easier to do. The advantage of breathing meditation is that we can do it anywhere. Engaging the seven-point posture helps mentally center yourself, but isn't absolutely essential in order to benefit from the exercise.

Meditation on Appreciation

By practicing this contemplative meditation that takes just a few minutes a day, you will begin to explore your mind in depth and develop a more refined perception of yourself. You'll attentively observe what is going on inside you with an opening to overcome anger, forgive yourself, and find a sense of calm and peace of mind.

This description of the Meditation on Appreciation is provided by His Eminence Gyalwa Dokhampa.

Meditation on Appreciation

1. Close your eyes and bring your thoughts into the present moment, reflecting on what is positive in your life right now. Start with your body, then slowly expand the circle to include your family and friends, your job, your community, and the world. When we aren't aware of what we already have, we tend to be dissatisfied in some way, focusing instead on what we think is missing from our life. We often have so much more than we think we do.

2. Start by thinking about your physical health; the simple fact that you are able to see and hear should be appreciated. Next, feel gratitude for having family and friends. We are fortunate to have people who love us unconditionally. Then expand your appreciation toward the world: good people exist to benefit others because the world exists.

3. All you need for this meditation is a quiet space, either at the beginning or end of the day. It doesn't matter what you are wearing, but comfortable clothes will reflect your comfortable mind. Sit in a chair or somewhere you feel alert and at ease; it doesn't matter where, and there's no need to be attached to a particular place or room.

4. Spend a couple of minutes focusing on your breath. Breathe gently and easily from your belly. Notice the breath, notice your belly rising and falling. Find a natural pace that's right for you. Contemplate and appreciate without clinging, without feeding attachment.

- Appreciate your body and whatever degree of health you have.

- Appreciate the wonderful people in your life who are kind to you and support you.

- Appreciate what you do—your career, your lifestyle, your community, and beyond.

5. Develop your personal sense of satisfaction. After all, what is happiness other than satisfaction? Go into as much detail as you like. Appreciate anything that comes to mind for what it is, simply and without any expectations or conditions.

Benefits

In the words of His Eminence Gyalwa Dokhampa, "To begin or end the day with appreciation may sound simplistic, but it works, providing an uplifting or calming effect after a difficult day. It is not about wearing rose-tinted glasses but finding the good in our lives or looking at situations from different angles—turning challenges into opportunities, for example."

Self-Reflection Meditation: Self-Knowledge and Altruism

This fourth and final exercise will be of continual use to you as you guide your child. You can use it with your child as soon as you feel she is mature enough for it.

Self-Reflection Meditation

In this meditation, which is done with closed eyes, you'll reflect on what you have done so far in your life. It helps to understand the situations you are experiencing in the moment and to accept that it is your own actions that led you here. You reflect on the kind of person you have become—how did you behave and react when you were a child or teenager; what did you do last year, last month, or just this morning? There is no such thing as a good or bad person here, as the true nature of being is always pure, but you can reflect on your actions and reactions.

1. It is helpful to look beyond any labels like "mother," "husband," or "boss" with the people in your life. Allow yourself to see them simply as human beings who also want happiness.

2. Then reflect on how you would like to be treated by others and how you treat the people in your life. Think about love, appreciation, respect, forgiveness, understanding, kindness, and compassion. Just as it takes two hands to clap, people tend to treat us with love, kindness, understanding, tolerance, and acceptance when we do so in kind.

3. Ask yourself directly: "What is happening in my life?" If you are feeling ill at ease in your day-to-day life, this question can help you to understand the cause.

We can sometimes get on our high horse when it comes to how we think of others. We might think that we are always right and that our partner, our boss, or anyone else is wrong, but this only makes life harder. Use this meditation as a form of mentally bending.

Benefits

This meditation works to develop self-knowledge and altruism. We realize that other people want to be respected and listened to just as we do. The more we are able to show respect and compassion for others, the more they will show the same for us. In matters of opinion, nobody is right or wrong, but when we impose our ideas on other people rather than taking theirs into consideration, the result is that everybody is unhappy. It is essential for us to listen to others well, for us to be attentive and understanding.

It is our hope that by practicing these four meditations you will be able to achieve some degree of transformation in your mind, however small. And if you begin to understand the way your mind works, this will not only help you to be happier, but your children and whole family will benefit as well. You will no longer depend on external circumstances to thrive, because you will be more comfortable with yourself. You will experience a fullness that can only come from within you.

PART TWO

MEDITATION

FOR YOUR CHILD

You now understand the basic principles and benefits of meditation. If you have started to practice yourself, it will only be easier to get your child meditating as well. In this part, you'll find out about the myriad benefits of meditation for your child—and for your family.

4 Meditation Starting at Age Three

The exercises in this book have been chosen for their simplicity, but they are so profound that they can be practiced our whole lives.

The First Steps

Most parents think that children are too young to meditate. How can they understand something that even adults have difficulty with? But in reality, young children are closer to their innate nature, and they are at the age where everything is possible. This means that any child is capable of learning the basics of meditation.

Getting Acquainted with Meditation

However, let's not go to the other extreme and think that your child is going to be able to find mental calm in just a few sessions. This is a project for a lifetime! The idea is to get your child acquainted with solid introductory practices to put her on this path. Children tend to take to meditation and they enjoy it because they sense its positive effects, and most of all, it's fun!

Louise was a very agitated three-and-a-half-year-old. She scootered frenetically in the schoolyard and would run in circles around the couch at home. Her teacher described her as a "difficult child." She had lots of little tantrums and cried at the least frustration. Her mother didn't know what to do anymore—she was at the point of exhaustion. Every night, her mother or godmother would read Louise a story at bedtime. But this was not enough to calm her down, and she had frequent nightmares. She would sleep badly and, because she had not gotten enough rest, in the morning she would be more frustrated and agitated than before. It was a vicious circle.

Louise was left with her grandmother for a month when her parents went abroad. After the first few days, the grandmother, who was feeling overwhelmed, began to wonder how she was going to keep up with this frantic pace for four weeks. The grandmother was a meditator with a regular practice, and she had experienced the benefits for herself. She started having Louise do three deep breaths in the meditation posture (with her legs crossed and back straight) every night before she went to sleep. She was astounded to see that Louise really took the whole thing seriously. She did her best to concentrate and would ask her grandmother if her posture was correct and if her belly was moving up and down properly. Every evening they did this exercise together— along with Louise's little teddy bear. A few days later, Louise's grandmother asked her if she had slept well, and Louise said, "Yes, I slept better." One day about a week later, her grandmother was in a hurry at bedtime and was about to skip the three breaths. She was surprised when Louise reminded her it was time to do the exercise! From then on, Louise would take her grandmother's hand and say to her, "Come on, Grandma, let's do the breaths." Louise had fun with the exercise, but she also could see how much it helped her. She was sleeping better and having better days at school. She was a much happier little girl.

Meditation Is Possible from Childhood On

Louise's experience shows that it is possible to make a three-year-old child aware of the potential of meditation. Even if she stops meditating as she grows up, she'll still remember the experience and will know that it is a way to soothe herself or shift negative states of mind.

Louise's example shows that the role of the guide is very important. The practice was successful because her grandmother took the time to do the exercise with her and had confidence in the effectiveness of the method.

The fundamental role of parents is to provide their children with a solid foundation as they grow up. By providing them with the tools they need to train their minds, you will help them to be happy and build a calmer and balanced life.

Resources for a Lifetime

Providing an introduction to authentic meditation is a way for parents to share special moments—profound and creative— with their children. Using very simple exercises, parents can give their children a taste of meditation practice and help them develop the habit of meditating. Practicing these exercises daily will provide children with resources that they can draw on for their whole lives.

5 The Benefits of Meditation for Your Child

Psychologist and clinician Jeanne Siaud-Facchin said, "The body is a very useful place to start, because it will always be there!" Focusing on the body is a completely natural starting point in teaching a child to meditate. In this chapter you will begin by helping your child to pay attention to the breath.

Breathing: A Key to the Body

In the same natural way that yawning and stretching enable your child to become more aware of her body and release tension caused by anger or frustration, the movement of the breath is the foundation for meditation. Becoming aware of the breath—that is, learning to put your attention on the air entering your nose, which swells the belly and then empties the belly—will attune your child more closely to her natural body movements and refine her perception of how the different parts of the body work together. And this in turn will bring her to a clearer perception of the external world and other people. At about three years old, a child begins to develop her personality in a new way—turning more outward, toward others, and beginning the process of socialization.

At this point, using direct experience to develop her perception of her body will help foster a harmonious relationship with the world.

Breathing is one of the first internal movements that can be seen. Seated in a cross-legged position, holding his teddy bear against his belly, it's easy for a child to see the little stuffed animal move up and down as he breathes. Such movements fascinate children, and they want to repeat the experience again and again. This begins to work around the age of three. Later on, around the age of five, a child becomes capable of relating the pulse to his breathing. After a race, for example, he will be intrigued by how his chest heaves or his neck throbs. He will get a kick out of placing his fingers on his neck to feel his pulse gradually slowing down. All these experiences help a child to know his body better and can be tremendously reassuring. In the same way, teaching a child to concentrate on his breath helps him to find calm in a natural way. He will experience his breathing slowing down little by little as agitation subsides and a breathing rhythm close to that of sleep takes over. He will fall asleep more peacefully as he feels this sense of calm coming over him. And when he sleeps more peacefully, he will recuperate better from the day and generally have more energy.

Stress Reduction

People tend to overdo the idea that childhood is a joyful, carefree time. While children don't have to work and don't have bills to pay, even little children have their anxieties and concerns and are subject to stress. Most of what troubles them comes from the outside, but they can also come from the inside—for example, a young child can feel pressure from family demands that they sense are being imposed on them (most often unintentionally by the parents).

Your little two-year-old can feel stressed because she feels you are not with her enough. When she goes off to preschool, being away from you can be a major source of anxiety. Parents who are quite successful professionally often have very high expectations for their little ones, and their children can sense this and experience it as a burden.

In recent years, teachers have noticed that more and more students have way too many extracurricular activities and don't really have time to relax. A child who starts to complain about this, or refuses to carry on with them, sends a clear signal to his parents about his level of stress. Your child can also experience increased stress from tuning in to your adult worries. He might take on a share of your anxiety and get upset by situations that shouldn't be his problem at all. A divorce, even one that unfolds in the smoothest possible way, means the child's protective family cocoon is undergoing a change, which can cause a great deal of anxiety.

It is not always easy to recognize the symptoms of stress in a child. Short-term changes in behavior like sudden sadness, trouble sleeping, or bedwetting are often signs of anxiety. Some children might start getting stomachaches or headaches. Others might have trouble concentrating at school. Younger children can react by developing new habits such as sucking their thumb or twisting their hair between their fingers. Older children can start lying or defying their parents' authority. A stressed child might see her grades start to fall in school.

Benefits for your Child's Emotions

What Are Emotions Good For?

Joy, anger, love, sadness, disgust—these emotions are at the core of our sense of self. They are the expression of the life within us, which is why it is essential that we identify them and learn to express them. And this is what a child of three or four is gradually learning to do: recognizing his emotions and naming them so he can express them. Crying, screaming, and trembling are some of the releases for the inevitable tensions of life and can help him to recover from hurt, fear, or anger.

Let's take fear, for example. When fear first arises, adrenaline is secreted and the heart rate accelerates. Next, the body tenses as we mobilize our maximum energy in order to deal with the situation. Finally, the energy is discharged and calm returns; once the danger has passed, the body returns to its basic equilibrium. Crying and trembling can occur when tension is released. If you know how to accept your child's emotions, and if you give your child the space to express them, she will feel more secure within herself—which is critical for building a stable personality. Getting through these kinds of difficulties mindfully will make her a more resilient person. This is exactly what you want as a parent.

Calming Down in Order to Verbalize

As we mentioned earlier, placing your attention on the breath allows you to find calm fairly quickly. After your child has come down from a bout of anger, you can encourage him to take a few conscious breaths in order to regain inner calm. Those breaths will help him to put words to the emotions he has just weathered. This is a skill that will accompany him through his entire life. Later on, he will be able to anticipate episodes of anger or other negative emotions and see them as they arise. Paying attention to the breath will help him perceive emotions clearly and move through them with greater equanimity.

Training Little Seekers of the Positive

One way of anchoring positive emotions such as happiness and love in your child's memory is to ask her to recount her day at school with an emphasis on identifying positive things. That is what we do in the Meditation on Appreciation that we will describe in detail a little later on. The exercise helps frustration, anger, and sadness go away. Instead of wallowing in negative emotions, you allow them to pass through you; they are experienced without too much drama and then are gradually forgotten! Your child can then put the emphasis on what brings her joy and happiness. Working with your child in this way can turn her into a little "seeker of the positive" no matter what circumstances she faces, including moments of anger or grief, and will serve her throughout her life.

How Meditation Can Help Your Child Succeed in School

Improved Concentration

Meditation is a wonderful tool for training your child to learn how to focus his attention and concentrate. It works very simply: while practicing the Meditation on the Breath, your child rests his attention on the in-breath and out-breath and is then completely present to himself and to the movements of his body. Like that, your child can be completely present and receptive at school and is better able to concentrate.

Researchers from the University of New South Wales in Australia carried out a study on children diagnosed with attention deficit disorder and hyperactivity. For six weeks, the parents of these children did six sessions of meditation a week with them. At the end of this period, they observed that their children were sleeping better, felt less agitated, and concentrated better in school, partly because they got involved in fewer conflicts with their friends. As for the parents, they reported feeling happier, less stressed, and better able to manage their children's behavior.

Greater Self-Confidence and Better Grades

A child who practices the Meditation on the Breath will improve her knowledge and awareness of her body, and little by little, she will come to experience her body as an ally and a source of well-being. Meditation strengthens self-esteem and promotes self-confidence. This is very useful when a child is being graded, tested, or quizzed, and later on, taking important examinations. The self-esteem fostered by a meditation practice will enable your child to feel less stressed about grades, have a positive attitude, and be more conscious of her potential. Another challenge children encounter is pop quizzes or surprise tests in class. These can be intimidating, but if your child meditates, she will be able to put her attention on the breath, and that will calm her nerves and allow her to access her knowledge more readily.

Improvement in Memory

Studies conducted at the Centre for Studies on Human Stress in Montreal have demonstrated that when stress hormones are secreted in either too large or too small amounts, our ability to learn and to retain new information is reduced. Your child's meditation practice will help regulate stress. Attention to the breath brings about mental calm, and the Meditation on Appreciation diminishes negative thinking, so the nervous system is soothed and the stress is contained. What emerges is an alert quality, which we can think of as "positive stress," the level of stress that best brings out our potential, including our memory.

If you give your child the opportunity to start meditating early in his life, he will be rewarded with improved circulation of energy in his body and brain, especially when he practices the breathing exercises. This will reduce physical and psychological tension and stress. When you make a routine of the Meditation on the Breath, your child will learn to detach from exaggerated worries and be able to retain a greater sense of inner space. Bad moods will be less frequent, and he will be more attuned to the positive things in life. In the long term, your child will be better able to fend off the negative effects of stress on his immune system and maintain good health. He will be less affected by troubles and without doubt be happier and healthier.

6 Introduction to the Yupsi Method

This part of the book will introduce you to our method of meditation and mind training for children. It begins with a test in altruism that takes the form of a game, and it is then followed by establishing a nightly bedtime routine. To help with this, we have provided a recording of the "Yupsi Song," the tales in this book, and the meditation exercises at www.shambhala.com/magicofmeditation.

Yupsi the Little Dragon and the Evening Routine

Yupsi the Little Dragon will be your child's companion as she discovers mind training. By reading the tales and doing the meditation exercises with Yupsi, your child will discover the benefits of concentration accompanied by compassion. That is the little seed that this book hopes to plant in the deepest level of your child's heart.

Yupsi is a kind and inspiring dragon your child will become fond of. In the eight Yupsi tales, you will notice that although the dragon appears in various guises, Yupsi remains reliably the same.

In some ways Yupsi is like a guardian angel, but Yupsi is also a spiritual friend. In the first of the teaching tales, the dragon shows the child what compassion is. Then, little by little, Yupsi draws the child into acting with compassion and love so your child's heart will gradually open toward others.

Your child will get to know Yupsi and get into the habit of calling on and concentrating on the dragon. When you reach the last teaching tale, your child will learn that the spiritual force the little dragon represents is within him as well. It is present in all children. Your child will learn that he can call upon this inner force at any time.

Yupsi is endowed with magic breath, like that of a mother who soothes her child's little wound by blowing on it. This is an introduction to the fundamental role of the breath. The exercises presented will familiarize your child with the breath and promote altruism.

The Evening Routine

In the whirlwind of our professional and family lives, we have less and less time to help our children deal with their daily lives. Yupsi the Little Dragon presents you with an easy-to-use working set of tools that requires just a few minutes every evening. This reassuring bedtime routine will turn out to be very important in your child's life. Maybe your child will take to this ritual right away, immediately sensing its benefits. But if she is less receptive, you will need more time and perseverance to get her to appreciate this short time of apparent inactivity.

The routine starts with reading a story about Yupsi's adventures, and it will be up to you to encourage interactive exchanges so your child can gradually assimilate the teaching.

After reading a story, play the music of the brief refrain, the "Yupsi Song" (track one of the recording). Sing along out loud with your child. The song opens the heart. The words are an integral part of the method, and your child will learn them quickly.

The song is the signal that it is time to assume the meditation posture. Instruct your child to sit on a cushion on the rug in his room, with a teddy bear or favorite blanket in his hands. It is amazing to see how naturally children take to this posture. And then do the exercises Meditation on the Breath and Meditation on Appreciation. You might think: "Wait a minute—the same meditations all the time? Wouldn't it be more fun to do a different exercise every night? My child would learn a lot more." That is actually not the case. If we changed the exercise every night, that might be entertaining, but your child would not learn the basic point of meditation, which is concentration on themselves. The aim here is not to provide variety but depth. We can never repeat the same exercise enough. The result comes from practice, from regularity and perseverance, not from providing distractions.

The routine ends with a dedication to all the children in the world.

Routine for Every Evening

- Opening the heart (reading a Yupsi story about compassion)

- The "Yupsi Song"

- Meditation on the Breath (three breaths)

- Meditation on Appreciation (appreciating this day)

- Dedication to All the Children in the World

The Eight Yupsi Stories

The tales you will read to your child are extremely simple. They make it possible to work on a particular emotion or a particular attitude toward others. The common denominator of these stories is opening the heart, which is designed to help develop compassion in your child. These tales must be read very attentively. As a parent, you will be able to feel how to introduce moments of silence into the reading, so that your child will have a chance to interact, ask questions, or make comments.

Each tale can be a point of departure for a discussion with your child on the subject Yupsi has brought up. You can ask questions such as "What are you feeling?" so that your child can gradually learn how to describe her emotions. Each story can be read several times; children love to hear their favorite stories repeated.

In the first few tales, Yupsi is completely separate from your child, but as you read further, he comes closer and closer to becoming a part of him or her. By the time you read the last story, your child will realize that the dragon is an integral part of himself.

Here are the main themes you will encounter in the Yupsi stories. Each story is preceded by a philosophical quotation.

The Blue Donkey Who Rode a Bike

In the tale of the blue donkey, your child will meet Yupsi for the first time. The little dragon shows the child how good it is to help other people, even if we don't know them. He explains how all beings want to be loved and helped—just as we do.

The Butterfly Kite

In this tale, Louise discovers the joy of sharing her kite with a child she doesn't know. She also learns, thanks to Yupsi, how enriching it is to give.

Trouble in the Land of the Bees

This tale explores the theme of the differences between people—some of whom seem to be more talented than others. Your child will learn that it is not helpful to get stuck on those sorts of details. For once again, we all want to be loved, and this is true no matter what our aptitudes are and no matter what our personality is like. This tale points out the negative role our ego can play and shows the importance of managing emotions such as anger, jealousy, and envy.

The Snowshoe Hare Caught in a Frozen Waterfall

The themes in this story are helping one another, the efficiency of team-work, and loyalty. All the animals of the forest, with Yupsi's encouragement, show their courage in saving the little hare. The emotion that comes up here is fear—that of the hare who is in danger at the bottom of a hole in the ice, and also that of the buck who fears that he will not be able to save his friend.

The Child from Ladakh

This tale has your child dream that she is flying all the way to India. But it is not the land of the maharajas that she discovers, but rather the northern part of India that is very close to the Tibetan border. Yupsi introduces your child to a little Ladakhi boy, who is unable to go to school. Your child will develop altruistic feelings toward the Ladakhi boy, and understand how precious it is to be able to go to school.

The Child with the Bandage

In this tale, Yupsi travels to London. The focus of the tale is once again ego. The child depicted here manifests emotions like anger and aggression mixed with vanity—the pretty little girl does not want to be seen with the nasty-looking little boy whose head is covered with bandages. Yupsi teaches her not to make hasty judgments and to feel compassion for the little boy.

The Wild Kittens

This tale is about compassion for animals. Animals are very sensitive creatures that deserve the same consideration as human beings. In no way are they to be seen as toys for children. That's what Yupsi makes your child understand through this story. If you like, you can even make use of this story as a way of introducing your child to the tragedy of animal abuse.

The Via Ferrata of Joy

This last tale is the culmination of the preceding stories. Yupsi helps your child realize that he exists within him or her—and always will. This story deals with the emotions of fear and anxiety. The point here is for your child to develop self-confidence. Yupsi shows your child that he possesses an inner force that he will have to develop over his whole life—and that meditation can help him to do this.

Summary

Through the Yupsi stories, your child will learn how to:

- Put a name to her emotions

- Sort out the various emotions he feels during his adventures with Yupsi

- Ask herself questions about her own emotions

- Receive the benefits of altruism by opening his heart

Reflecting on these tales with your child will give her a good base for dealing with anxiety, depression, aggression, and other difficulties in life. Remember that your attitude as a parent plays a fundamental role in stimulating the emotional intelligence of your child. For that reason we should do our very best to be emotionally intelligent parents!

The "Yupsi Song"

Your child has the right to a little recreation, and that's why we created the "Yupsi Song." This light and cheerful song is intentionally repetitive so that your child can learn it by heart and sing it anytime during the day. The children we worked with who tried out the song learned it quickly and didn't want to stop singing it. And this is a very good thing, because the words of the song—which are simple but repeat the words "heart," "help," and "happiness"—were conceived with an altruistic education in mind. Such an education goes beyond the meditation cushion into all moments in your child's life.

Moreover, sound and chanting are an incredible support for meditation practice. From time immemorial, yogis and great meditators have used chants known as mantras, because they recognized the power of certain sounds. So let's go ahead and sing the "Yupsi Song"!

Just like Yupsi the Little Dragon
Open your eyes
Open your heart
You will see how good it is
To help others
That is happiness!

The Meditation on the Breath and the Meditation on Appreciation

We have included several meditations here so you can choose ones that suit the age of your child. The littlest ones will be proud to do the three breaths and to reflect on the good things that have happened to them during the day; that is enough at their age. What counts is regularity, repetition of the meditation every evening. As time goes on, you can develop and enrich your child's practice.

The meditations suggested for older children are basically the same as the ones that you, as adults, were asked to practice at the end of part 1, but of course they are somewhat simplified. As with the very little ones, it is a good idea to keep repeating the same exercise and gradually make it longer. For very young children, a good length is two minutes, then three minutes. Then you can go to twenty minutes for teenagers, and adults can do forty-five minutes or even longer if they want.

If you find yourself exhausted at the end of the day, you can practice for five minutes in the evening with your child: relax and observe your breathing going in and out, then think with gratitude and appreciation about the good things that happened to you during the day. This cannot fail to bring you a sense of well-being and reduce your feelings of stress. The sharing that will be created by practicing evening after evening with your child will be as satisfying for you as it will be for her.

Dedication to All the Children in the World

The evening ritual should end without fail with a dedication to all the children in the world. This will complete the opening of the heart to a sense of altruism. This is fundamental for stimulating emotional and relational intelligence.

If you happen to possess a Tibetan or Nepalese singing bowl, sounding it can be a pleasant way to finish your evening routine. The clear and open sound, long and gentle, can be very soothing for children at bedtime. But this is not essential.

The Gift Stickers

When parents modify their children's education, even a little, it is not rare for doubts to come up afterward. They wonder, was I right to have recommended that? Is this kind of education properly suited to my child? Will she be able to get the benefit of it? In order to help you confirm your intuition in this case, we have included the following test in the Yupsi method. It was inspired by an experiment in a preschool in Madison, Wisconsin, which we learned about from Matthieu Ricard.[1] The experiment was devised by the Center for Investigating Healthy Minds, founded by the psychologist and neuroscientist Richard Davidson.

Every morning for ten weeks, a group of children ages four and five years old were asked to lie down on their backs and pay close attention to the movements of their breath. They then repeated aloud this expression of their motivation: "May everything I think, everything I say, and everything I do cause others no harm but be helpful to them instead." And in the course of the day, their teachers would emphasize taking an altruistic approach.

Before beginning this experiment, the school principal asked her students to present gifts to four categories of other children: their best friend, a child they had never seen before, a visibly ailing child wearing a bandage on his forehead, and the child they liked the least. The result was clear immediately; almost all the gifts went to the best friends.

At the end of ten weeks of three sessions of thirty minutes a week, the researchers found that the children distributed their gifts much more equally among the different children. Confronted with these amazing results, the city of Madison asked Richard Davidson to extend his program to the town's other schools.

The test for the Yupsi method is similar; it is to be given for the first time the day your child begins the evening routine and for the second time after ten weeks of daily practice. So before reading the Yupsi tales, have your child complete the first test page.

Here is how we suggest you prepare the two pages for the tests. Take two photos of your child's best friend (one for each test page) and paste one of them on each page next to the gift box marked "photo" (page 58 and 100).

Then play the stickers game with your child. Have a sheet of stickers on hand, preferably the self-sticking kind. It doesn't matter what they depict. Children love to stick and re-stick stickers. Clearly explain to your child that Yupsi has brought a whole lot of gifts to be given out, and that your child can give them to whomever they want, without any restriction. Then just watch and see how your child decides to distribute the gifts. That will give you an idea of their initial tendencies.

At the end of a minimum of ten weeks, do the test again, using the second page. If you observe a change in the way the gifts are distributed, it means that Yupsi has accomplished his mission!

The Audio Download

As we have been emphasizing, consistency is key, as is your presence— if possible, your mindful presence, grounded in the here and now. That said, if it happens that you have to be away, the audio download (www.shambhala.com/magicofmeditation) can somewhat replace you. But you can also listen to it with your child.

The audio consists of twelve tracks that can be explored as is appropriate to your child's age and level of progress.

TRACK ONE: The "Yupsi Song"
Within the framework of the routine, listen to the "Yupsi Song" every evening, at least at the beginning, so you can learn it along with your child and sing it with her. You should listen to the song just after reading the Yupsi tale, while sitting in the meditation posture on a cushion.

TRACK TWO: Every Evening, Do What Yupsi Does (Meditation for Young Children, Starting at Age Three)
After having listened to a tale, your child will be asked to listen to two texts to initiate her into meditation. This includes:

- The Lotus (or Cross-Legged) Position
- Three-Breath Meditation
- Meditation on Appreciation
- Dedication to All the Children in the World

TRACK THREE: Meditation for Older Kids, Starting at Age Five
(or according to your child's progress)
These are meditations for older children, which they would do just after listening to a tale. Here are the contents:

- Meditation on the Breath: White Light and Black Smoke
- Meditation on Appreciation
- Dedication to All the Children in the World

TRACK FOUR: Walking Meditation (for Ages Five and Up)
(or according to your child's interest)
Here we present walking meditation. Your child only needs to listen to the audio and match their step to the rhythm of the walk as it is presented there.

TRACKS FIVE TO TWELVE: The Eight Yupsi Stories
Each evening your child will pick which one of the eight Yupsi tales they want to listen to.

That's it! You're ready to start meditating with your child. There is nothing left to do now but experience those special moments with her that will enrich and deepen your relationship—joyfully and with a light heart!

PART THREE

THE YUPSI STORIES

AND MEDITATIONS

This part of the book includes the Gift Stickers Test, the meditations, and the stories. Use these "scripts" as the basis for doing the program with your child, and follow the order given on page 45. Do the Gift Stickers Test with your child before beginning the Yupsi program and then again ten weeks later.

7 The Gift Stickers Test: Your Child's Initial Level of Compassion

Yupsi the Little Dragon lives in a galaxy different from our own in which everybody is happy. But since he really loves children, he often comes down to visit Earth in order to help them have a more joyful life.

Today Yupsi wants to play with you. He has brought you a whole lot of gifts so that you can give them away to others. So who are you going to give all these presents to? (Show the sheet of stickers.)

You can give them to your best friend, to a child you don't know, to a child who is sick or has had an accident, or to somebody in your class who you always find annoying.

Stick the stickers on the children's gift boxes. You don't have to give them to everybody, and you can stick on as many as you want. It's completely up to you!

Now count up the number of presents you have given each child and show the results on the side.

Your best friend

Total

Unknown child

Total

Sick child

Total

The child who annoys you the most

Total

8 Every Evening, Do What Yupsi Does

It's time for bed! As he does every evening, Yupsi the Little Dragon is going to concentrate for a little while on his magic breath before going to sleep and getting a good night's rest.

The Lotus (or Cross-Legged) Position

First, take your teddy bear or your favorite blanket and put it in the same place as the child in the drawing has it.

1. Sit down in the lotus position on your favorite cushion. Your legs should be crossed with the left leg on the inside, closest to your body, and the right leg outside. You can also sit cross-legged, if you prefer.

2. Keep your back straight, like a stack of coins.

3. Keep your eyes open, looking downward.

4. Put your teddy bear or the little blanket against your lower belly and rest your hands on your thighs.

Three-Breath Meditation

1. Observe your breath. . . . When you breathe in slowly, your belly swells. . . . You can feel your teddy bear move forward. Hold your breath in your belly for a moment. . . . Now you breathe out and your belly empties and goes flat. . . . You can feel the bear moving back inward.

2. Concentrate carefully on your breath and your little bear. Follow the movement of the little bear back and forth with your breath.

3. Breathe in slowly. You feel your belly swelling and your little bear moving forward. Hold your breath in your belly for a second. Now breathe out, and your belly empties and flattens, and you feel your little bear moving back inward.

4. Breathe in slowly again. You feel your belly swelling and your little bear moving forward. Hold your breath for a second in your belly. Now breathe out, and your belly empties and flattens and you feel your little bear moving back inward.

Meditation on Appreciation

1. Now you can remain on your cushion or sit on the edge of your bed and close your eyes. Think of everything that happened to you today that was good.

2. Think of your teacher and everything she did for you. . . . Think of your mommy who helped you and of your best friend, who you played with in the park or in the schoolyard. . . . Think of everything that happened to you today that was good. . . .

3. Remain silent for a moment to appreciate all that. . . .

You're all done!

Tell me how it went. Do you feel better?

Dedication to All the Children in the World

Yupsi now expresses his loving wishes for you and for all the children in the world. You too can wish from the bottom of your heart for all the children in the world to be happy. Say aloud, "I want all the children in the world to be happy."

Good night!

9 The Yupsi Stories

Follow the adventures of Yupsi the Little Dragon and all his friends!

THE BLUE DONKEY WHO RODE A BIKE

You do good for yourself by being concerned for others.

—HIS HOLINESS GYALWANG DRUKPA

One beautiful, sunny day, Yupsi decided to go for a walk in the forest.

As he was going along the road that winds among the trees, he saw a blue donkey sitting on the ground, and there was a bicycle lying next to him in the grass. The donkey seemed very sad, probably because one of his bike tires was completely flat.

Yupsi, who had never seen a blue donkey, thought he was very strange, but he decided to go talk to him anyway.

"Hi, beautiful blue donkey," Yupsi

said. "What are you doing sitting on the ground there? Tell me a little about what is making you sad."

"I was going to the nearby village to be in a bike race," the blue donkey explained, snuffling noisily, "when suddenly I got a flat tire, right there on the road. I tried to fix it, but my tire pump broke. My bike won't work anymore. No more bike, no more race—that's why I'm so sad."

"Do you know that dragons have very powerful breath?" Yupsi replied.

"So what?" answered the blue donkey with a sob.

"Well, it so happens that I'm a dragon, and I bet that I can blow your tire up! But first we'll have to take this out." Leaning over the bike, Yupsi pulled a little pointy piece of metal out of the tire and proclaimed, "Look, it's this nasty nail that gave you the flat tire!"

All it took was a little bit of very sticky dragon spit to plug the hole in the tire. The repair was almost done. The blue donkey watched the whole scene with admiration in his eyes. All his tears had dried up.

There was nothing left to do but fix the tire, and Yupsi blew it back up with just one big puff. Thanks to Yupsi's magic breath, the bike was all ready to go!

"Oh, you fixed my bike!" the blue donkey shouted, beside himself with joy. "Thank you, Yupsi! Now, because of you I'm going to be in the race after all."

With these words, he kissed the little dragon's snout as a thank-you and went off down the road, singing as he went along through the forest.

Seeing the blue donkey's joy, Yupsi suddenly felt very light and very happy.

Just like Yupsi the Little Dragon

Open your eyes

Open your heart

You will see how good it is

To help others

That is happiness!

Now it's time for the three breaths! You can find the meditation on page 60 (for the little ones) and page 93 (for the older ones).

THE BUTTERFLY KITE

Only love knows the secret of enriching itself by giving.

—SOCRATES

One day when Yupsi the Little Dragon was walking around on Earth, he saw a little girl in a playground who looked sad.

In her hands she had a very beautiful kite made of pink silk that was in the shape of a butterfly. Her whole life she had dreamed about owning a kite like this, and her mother had just brought her this one back from a trip to Beijing, China.

Yupsi went up to her and said, "Hi, Louise" (because he could always guess the first name of any child he met). "You really have the most beautiful kite in the world. So why are you making such a sad face?"

"There's not enough wind today," Louise replied, "so I'm upset because my kite won't fly."

A little boy came along. He looked at the kite with his eyes wide with wonder, because he had never seen such a beautiful kite in his life.

Seeing this, Yupsi said to Louise: "Since you're not playing with your kite, could you lend it to this little boy? His name is Max. You'll see how nice it feels to make someone happy."

"No way," replied the little girl, "it's my kite and I'm going to keep it."

When Yupsi started to insist, Louise got angry and stamped her foot. "No, it's mine!" she said. "It's mine!"

So the dragon said to her gently: "If you don't want to lend Max your kite, at least share it with him and the two of you can play together."

Louise thought about it. After a few seconds a big smile appeared on her face. She skipped over to where Max was standing and asked him to come play with her. The little boy's eyes got very bright. He was really happy with this idea!

To make it possible for both Louise and Max to play with the kite, Yupsi used his magic breath. He pointed his nostrils to the sky, and a lovely wind began to blow over the playground. The big pink butterfly rose in the air and began to fly. The children ran after it, laughing. It was wonderful to see them having fun together. Their hearts were full of joy.

After a while, Louise got tired and stopped running. She let Max play with the kite all by himself. She watched him having fun running around like mad and flying the pink silk butterfly. She realized then how happy it was making Max to fly the butterfly. He seemed even happier than she was herself to have a kite. Right on the spot, she decided to give it to him. Yes, she was going to give Max her kite! And at this thought, she felt her heart jump for joy inside her.

Seeing the two children smiling and happy, Yupsi felt very light and very happy.

Just like Yupsi the Little Dragon
Open your eyes
Open your heart
You will see how good it is
To help others
That is happiness!

Now it's time for the three breaths. You can find the meditation on page 60 (for the little ones) and page 93 (for the older ones).

TROUBLE IN THE LAND OF THE BEES

All unhappiness comes from love of self, and all happiness comes from the
altruistic heart.

—SHANTIDEVA

Leah was a young and pretty bee in Provence, France, and she was very
proud of her splendid dress that had stripes of brown, orange, and pale
yellow. She was a nectar bee; it was her job to bring nectar back to the
hive from the flowers that she drew it from. And there were plenty of
flowers in Provence that were good for making honey. Leah could gather
nectar from all kinds of plants, such as rapeseed, thyme, lime blossom,
chestnut, lavender, and acacia. But she chose to gather her harvest from
the white flowers of the almond tree only, because almond blossoms are
the most delicate of all.

Every morning she prepared herself. She carefully brushed her
wings with her slender, delicate feet. This is because her two pairs of
wings had to be perfectly smooth and clean so they could beat perfectly when she flew. Sometimes she would run across Yupsi the Little
Dragon, whose bee friends would give him honey.

Leah left the hive very early in the morning to go and land on
the most beautiful almond flowers in the area. Working very hard, she
would fill the fold in the front of her dress with the precious nectar,
which she then carried back to the hive.

Unfortunately, her days were always ruined by Clara, another bee
who was very jealous of her and was constantly pestering her. When
Leah picked out a beautiful almond flower, Clara immediately appeared
and gave the flower a bump so that she too could perch on the same one.

And since the flower was too small for two, it swayed back and forth and forced both bees to fly away. Then Leah would have to fly off to find another flower. But Clara was always there to give a push so she could perch on her flower with her.

"Stop following me!" Leah shouted at her.

"Don't make such a big fuss. Go and find yourself another flower," Clara replied.

"Do you know I have to make at least ten trips a day to bring nectar back to the hive? And you're always there, slowing me down!" Leah exclaimed.

"But you're the only one who knows how to find such beautiful flowers," Clara wailed. "Let me just get the nectar out of this one, and go find another one for yourself."

Every day they fought like this over the almond flowers. Finally, Leah had had enough of it. She made up her mind that Clara was her worst enemy, and she began trying to figure out how she could get rid of her once and for all.

One gorgeous morning, Leah was busy gathering her precious harvest. She was so wrapped up in her work that she didn't see a nasty red crab spider approaching. Now, the spider is a very dangerous animal for bees. It catches them in its sticky web and eats them up. That morning the spider was laying in ambush, watching Leah gathering nectar. After a while it wove a strong net between two almond flowers, using very solid and sticky threads of silk. Then it waited patiently for Leah to decide to change from one flower to another. When Leah flew off at her top speed in order to avoid wasting any time, the little bee crashed violently into the spider's web. She was caught in a trap of silken threads! No doubt about it, the spider was going to eat her up!

Following her usual habit, Clara had followed Leah from flower to flower. It didn't take her long to see that Leah was in serious danger.

What could she do to help? She decided to go get Yupsi, because she couldn't do anything against a big spider all by herself. She flew as fast as she could to where Yupsi was staying and asked him to come help Leah. They went off together to help her. When they got to the spider's web, Leah was still struggling to escape.

Immediately, Yupsi started breathing out little flames to make the spider, who was terrified of fire, back off. While this was happening, Clara used her powerful jaws to cut through the silk threads. She kept cutting until she had Leah completely free of the web. Then Clara set Leah gently down on Yupsi's back, for in the meantime the little bee had fainted. Together they took her back to the hive.

When Leah came to, the first bee she saw was Clara. Seeing Clara's smile, Leah knew she was the one who had saved her life. She suddenly felt a bit ashamed. She didn't feel good about always trying to keep the most beautiful almond flowers for herself, when really she could have helped Clara to find the best nectar too and shared the harvest with her. Yes, indeed, she said to herself, I have really been selfish.

From this day on, things changed. Every morning, Leah called Clara to go with her so she could show her the most beautiful flowers that she could gather the sweetest nectar from. Together they made a team. Between the two of them, they brought the most nectar back to the hive of all the bees. On top of that, Leah knew she could depend on Clara, because she had a very good eye for spotting spiders hiding among the flowers. With Clara, Leah was no longer in danger.

Yupsi was feeling very light and very happy since the two bees had become friends and had finally learned to love and appreciate the differences between them. Thanks to them, the hive was producing more honey than ever for little honey lovers, and Yupsi himself was licking his chops.

Just like Yupsi the Little Dragon
Open your eyes
Open your heart
You will see how good it is
To help others
That is happiness!

Now it's time for the three breaths! You can find the meditation on page 60 (for the little ones) and page 93 (for the older ones).

THE SNOWSHOE HARE CAUGHT IN A FROZEN WATERFALL

When we perform positive actions motivated by kindness, altruism, and empathy, we feel fully ourselves.

—*DU BONHEUR* (HAPPINESS), FRÉDÉRIC LENOIR

Winter had arrived on Earth and the cold had covered all the mountains with a thick coating of white snow. Pom-pom, a snowshoe hare who could change his color, had just come out of his burrow and was enjoying himself jumping around in the snow and catching the flakes that whirled around above his head. Since it was winter, Pom-pom had lost his gray-brown summertime fur and had become completely white, so he blended in with the snow.

With the help of his back paws that had the shape of snowshoes, he could jump around to his heart's content without sinking in the powdery snow. And he was really going at it! But all of a sudden he landed on a very hard sheet of ice and began to slip. He felt unable to stop himself. He slid and he slid and he kept sliding till he landed on a totally frozen waterfall. Lying on his side with his feet flailing in the air, Pom-pom continued to slide. One second he was spinning around on the frozen mirror, the next second he was shooting downward like a lightning bolt. Finally, he hit a little bump in the ice and flew up into the air. He came back down just on the edge of a hollow in the ice, a rather deep hole into which he suddenly disappeared with a long piercing cry. There he was, a prisoner of the waterfall!

Just by chance, Zooari the Little Buck had seen the whole incident—the terrifying slide down the waterfall and the fall into the icy hole. He bounded over the fresh snow till he got close to the hollow that Pom-pom had disappeared into. He bent a little over the edge to catch a glimpse down into it. There with relief he saw the snowshoe hare wedged at the bottom, flailing about, trying to jump out of the hole.

"Don't worry, Pom-pom," Zooari shouted down to him, "I'll go get help to get you out of there!"

And without waiting, he galloped away. He hadn't gone far when, on a slope of fresh snow, he ran across Yupsi, who was sledding around on the hillside, laughing and apparently having a really great time.

Zooari shouted to him: "Yupsi, I really need you. Pom-pom has fallen into a hole in the ice. How can we help him?"

"First of all, stay calm," said Yupsi, and the little dragon began to think. "There, I've got it. I have an idea, but it's going to take a lot of help. Go find your friends and tell them to meet by the waterfall, near the place where our friend Pom-pom is trapped. Also tell them to bring with them all the wood they find on the way. I think that might turn out to be very helpful!"

No sooner said than done. Zooari alerted all the animals and gave them Yupsi's message. It was not long before the fox, the weasel, the mountain goat, the white ermine, and the lynx were all by the side of the waterfall loaded with branches of wood of all sizes.

Yupsi quickly organized the rescue party. With his front paws he got a good hold on the trunk of a big tree, and then he pointed his long reptilian tail in the direction of the hole in the ice from which the cries of the trapped hare could be heard. His tail reached a short way into the hole, but it wasn't long enough to reach Pom-pom. Yupsi then asked the buck to go down along his back and to hang from the end of his tail to try to reach Pom-pom. But it wasn't enough!

Then it was the lynx's turn to slide down Yupsi's back, and then hang from the feet of the buck in order to get down still deeper into the hole. That still wasn't enough, so Yupsi asked the fox to climb down his tail and go all the way down till he was hanging from the lynx's paws. But there was still a short distance to go to reach Pom-pom. The courageous weasel went down next. He went carefully down along Yupsi's tail, then passing over the heads and bodies of all his friends, he finally ended up hanging firmly onto the paws of the fox. He felt his little claws touching the bottom of the hole. Pom-pom was finally able to climb up the backs of his friends, up the tail of the little dragon, and finally get out into the open air. He was saved! Then, one by one, his friends climbed back up to the surface.

Seeing all the animals shivering with cold after their team effort, Yupsi began to huff and puff with all his might with his magic breath

onto the pile of wood lying near the waterfall. The wood immediately caught fire. Huge flames mounted toward the sky and warmed up the little band of happy rescuers.

Thanks to his calmness and his courage, but especially owing to the teamwork of all the animals, Zooari the Buck had been able to help the snowshoe hare escape from the ice of the waterfall.

Then all the animals made a circle around the fire and danced with light and happy hearts, happy that they had listened to Yupsi and saved their friend.

Just like Yupsi the Little Dragon
Open your eyes
Open your heart
You will see how good it is
To help others
That is happiness!

Now it's time for the three breaths! You can find the meditation on page 60 (for the little ones) and page 93 (for the older ones).

THE CHILD FROM LADAKH

Leave more room for others in your heart.

—*THE RESTFUL MIND*, HIS EMINENCE GYALWA DOKHAMPA

Emma is a little girl who is never satisfied and who tends to get angry often and to cry and whimper till she gets her way. No matter how many times her mama explains to her that this doesn't do any good, Emma continues to behave that way anyhow.

One day Yupsi the Little Dragon, who knew her well, made her a strange offer:

"You cry a lot, my little Emma. You are unhappy, and I'm sure it's because you think you don't have enough toys. Would you like to become the happiest little girl on Earth?"

Emma nodded her head to say yes, so Yupsi continued:

"Then go ahead and climb up on my back. Since my breath is as powerful as the engine of a jet plane, I can make you fly. I am going to take you with me to see other children, and you'll see how you get to be just as happy as they are!"

Emma climbed up between the wings on Yupsi's back, and together the two of them flew for a long time over oceans and seas. They flew until they reached Ladakh, in northern India, in a region of very high mountains called the Himalayas. In Ladakh, the earth is so dry that almost nothing grows.

Yupsi and Emma finally arrived in Tiri, a small mountain village where a little boy named Tsering Dorje lived. He was a friend of Yupsi's. Even though he had very few toys in his home, Tsering Dorje seemed to be very happy. His parents did all they could for him. Every day they gave him plenty of food, and above all, plenty of love. His favorite toy was a little iron box that he pushed along with a stick. And when he went to take care of the beautiful pashmina goats that belonged to his family, the little box kept him company on the path and made sounds like soft music that helped gather his flock around him.

Tsering was very fond of his life in Ladakh, but he had one big regret. He was not able to go to school. The fact was that in his village, which was very isolated in the mountains, a school had never been built. So in order to get to a school, he would have to go to a town very far away from his village, and this would be too expensive for his parents. And anyway, his parents needed him to take care of the goats.

Emma made friends with Tsering right away. He taught her to find her way in the mountains, to listen for and recognize the songs of the birds, to read the patterns in the clouds and stars. Together they enjoyed the roasted barley porridge that Tsering's parents gave him for the midday meal. They also played together pushing the little iron box around.

Little by little, Emma began to realize how easy her life was and how lucky she was to be able to go to school each day. She promised herself to ask her parents how they might be able to help Tsering go to school one day, because he was very smart, and school might be able to change his life. It also occurred to her that she could ask her teacher and her classmates about it. Together they might be able to come up with an idea for raising money to build a school in Tsering's village.

All these ideas blossomed in Emma's heart and gave her a great deal of joy. She suddenly felt happy, very happy. She was the happiest little girl in the world!

But it was time to go home, because it was getting late. Yupsi promised Emma he would take her back to Ladakh sometime to see Tsering. So she climbed back on the dragon's back with her heart full of love and joy.

Just like Yupsi the Little Dragon
Open your eyes
Open your heart
You will see how good it is
To help others
That is happiness!

Now it's time for the three breaths! You can find the meditation on page 60 (for the little ones) and page 93 (for the older ones).

THE CHILD WITH THE BANDAGE

You should never judge people by their appearance.

—"THE PEASANT OF THE DANUBE," *FABLES*, JEAN DE LA FONTAINE

It was Sunday afternoon, and Maya was riding on her red scooter, which was ornamented with a beautiful purple horse's head. She had gotten her mom's permission to ride her scooter down their street to the local park. Of course she had had to promise to keep her helmet on the whole time, to definitely stay on the sidewalk, and above all, to be really careful when she crossed the street to get into the park. With her head full of these promises, Maya went speeding along, her heart light in her chest.

It was at that moment that a blue scooter passed her going very fast.

Maya sped up in order to catch up with it. When she came up beside it, Maya turned her head to see who was riding it and saw a little boy with a big bandage that came down from underneath his helmet and went across his whole forehead. He was wearing big, thick glasses and his face was covered with freckles. Maya found herself breaking out laughing at the sight of this funny-looking little boy. Here was a kid who obviously didn't know how to ride a scooter and who must have taken a tumble on the sidewalk just because of something like a little tree root!

"An idiot, this kid is really a total idiot," Maya thought. And she sped up some more in order to pass him. Then she heard a voice from behind her:

"Hey, wait up!" the little boy shouted to her. "My name is Archie, and I want to play with you!"

But Maya had no desire to play with this kid who really must be rather dumb, since he hadn't been able to avoid falling—and he might even make her fall herself. So she tried to go as fast as she could in order to leave him behind. But Archie, who actually handled his scooter quite well, caught up with her. He signaled to her to stop so they could talk. Maya felt herself getting angry. She stopped short and told him right to his face:

"You leave me alone. I don't want to play with you. It's easy to see you don't know how to ride a scooter, since you obviously keep falling."

"Hey, what are you talking about?" Archie replied. "Actually, I have really good balance, and I saw that you manage pretty well yourself. That's why I wanted to play with you in the park."

"Is that so? So then how do you explain that big ugly bandage you've got on your forehead? You must have fallen down, and that means you're hopeless as a scooter rider. Me, I don't play with such hopeless cases, and that's all there is to it!"

And with these words, Maya sped away on her scooter and rode off into the park. Rolling along the lanes of the park lit with springtime sun, she ran into Yupsi the Little Dragon, who was taking a rest, stretched out in the green, green grass.

"Hi, Yupsi," shouted Maya. "Beautiful day, isn't it?"

"So it is," replied Yupsi, "but not for everybody."

"I see," said Maya. "Something's bothering you. If you want to tell me about it, here I am. I'll be glad to listen."

Yupsi knew Maya well. He knew that she had a good heart. So he went ahead and spoke.

"I want to talk to you about a little boy who is feeling very bad today." Saying that, he blew with his magic breath, and it took the shape of a big white cloud, which became like a movie screen for Maya.

"I want to talk to you about Archie." And a little boy with lots of freckles appeared on the screen. Maya recognized him right away. Yupsi went on talking while the images continued on the screen. "Here's what happened to him. Two weeks ago, he was taking care of his little sister at their house. Since she was just beginning to walk, Archie was keeping an eye on her. But he went into the kitchen for a moment to get a glass of water. During that time she managed to climb up on the windowsill, and when Archie came back, he found her teetering on it, just about to tumble into space. Paying no attention to anything but his courageous heart, he leapt up and caught hold of her and pulled her back from the window, keeping his arms around her to protect her. As he was carrying out this heroic action, his head bumped into the radiator, and he injured his forehead. That big bandage that you saw is the mark of his courage."

Then the screen made of Yupsi's magic breath dissolved, and Maya's eyes were full of tears. She realized she had judged Archie unjustly. She was very sorry that she had been so mean to him. What could she do?

Yupsi looked at her tenderly, and with his big dragon paw, pointed to a blue scooter that could be seen moving among the lanes of the park. Maya didn't waste a second. She jumped on her scooter and rode off after Archie. She found the words to get him to forgive her for her mistake and for treating him unkindly. She also asked him to join in her games with her, and this brought a smile back to his face.

From a distance, Yupsi watched them talk, then break out laughing, and then move off together side by side on their little vehicles. Seeing the two children full of joy again, he felt very light and very happy.

Just like Yupsi the Little Dragon
Open your eyes
Open your heart
You will see how good it is
To help others
That is happiness!

Now it's time for the three breaths! You can find the meditation on page 60 (for the little ones) and page 93 (for the older ones).

THE WILD KITTENS

We have to put humans back into the heart of the animal world.

—*L'ANIMAL EST UNE PERSONNE* (AN ANIMAL IS A PERSON),

FRANZ-OLIVIER GIESBERT

As they very often did when they were on vacation at their grandfather's house, Louise and Ilam were playing in the shed just behind the farmhouse. This old lean-to also served as a dump, though the children always discovered many treasures when they played there.

While they were busy trying to get an old electric car out from where it was stuck between two huge cans, Louise thought she heard a small noise, squeaky and sad. It sounded like crying and was coming from some piled-up boxes of books.

"What could that be?" she asked herself. She was pretty sure that they were alone in the shed, and Ilam hadn't heard anything. And anyway, he was only interested in the little electric car.

"Come over here and help me," he called to his sister, "instead of fooling around by those boxes. The car is stuck!"

"Fine, okay," said Louise, coming back. "Do you think that car belonged to Papa?"

But the little cries came again—and this time, Ilam heard them too. The children ran over to the place behind the boxes where the cries were coming from.

There they found three gray kittens, meowing for their mother. They had just been born and were lying there on the hard earth floor, all bare and trembling, without any fur or anything to protect them.

"Oh! They are really creepy!" Ilam cried as he picked one up by the neck. "They look like rats, horrible little rats!" And he shook the kitten. Terrified, the kitten mewed louder and louder.

All of a sudden, Ilam dropped it, because he had seen the mother cat coming toward him, ready to spring. The two children ran and hid in their grandfather's car. From this vantage point, they watched the mother cat take her kittens one by one in her mouth by the back of their neck and move them to a safe place, behind the wood pile. All of them except the one Ilam had shaken. He lay alone there on the cold ground, mewing loudly, calling to his mother, who didn't seem interested in caring for him at all. In fact, she had disappeared, and the little creature was exhausting itself squealing constantly. From the little car, helpless, the children watched this scene, afraid that it would have a very bad ending.

Leaping up, Louise ran to the farmhouse to get some advice from her grandfather. He told her, "Louise, these are wild kittens. If you pet one or touch it, you leave your smell on it. The mother cat will probably abandon it. You shouldn't have touched it."

Louise didn't dare say that they had done worse than just touch the kitten. They had shaken it and dropped it. She was ashamed, but she did not want to tattle on her brother. She went back to the shed, almost in tears. By this time, Ilam was in a panic, because the little kitten, exhausted, lay stretched out on the ground and seemed to be dead. And the mother cat was gone once and for all.

"I can't think of any other solution but to call Yupsi," said Louise. "He's the only one who can help us."

The little girl set her mind strongly on Yupsi the Little Dragon, who arrived immediately with a beating of wings. He began by gently scolding Ilam for his bad behavior toward the little animal. Then quick-

ly he turned to the kitten, because it really needed help. He asked Ilam to take the little cat in his arms in order to warm it up, and he began to blow deep magic breaths. He blew gentle, long, and warm magic breaths on the little animal, and then licked its whole body. The kitten was warmed up again by this massage, and then it opened one eye and then the other. Ilam, laughing, kissed its little head. He was so happy to see it alive.

"This little cat will be counting on you from now on," Yupsi declared. "You will have to take care of it like you were its mama. You will have to feed it and give it lots of attention." Then he turned to look at Ilam and gave him a wink. Then he said, "Your first job is to find some milk for it, because it looks really hungry."

Yupsi had no sooner finished talking when the two children raced off to their grandfather's house, holding the little cat wrapped in their arms.

"For sure Grandpa will be able to help us feed our kitten," puffed the little boy, out of breath, to his sister. "We haven't got a second to lose. It's our responsibility now."

Louise went out on the porch to say goodbye to Yupsi, who was just about to take off into the air. She gave him a big wave and thanked him warmly. Yupsi smiled back at her. The brother and sister felt great happiness. For sure they were going to take good care of the kitten, and from then on they would show respect to all animals.

Just like Yupsi the Little Dragon
Open your eyes
Open your heart
You will see how good it is
To help others
That is happiness!

Now it's time for the three breaths! You can find the meditation on page 60 (for the little ones) and page 93 (for the older ones).

THE VIA FERRATA OF JOY

"Goodbye," said the fox. "And now here is my secret, a very simple secret: It is only with the heart that one can see rightly; what is essential is invisible to the eye."

—*THE LITTLE PRINCE*, ANTOINE DE SAINT-EXUPÉRY

That morning, the first rays of the sun did not hesitate to wake up Gaspard and Philomena, who were still totally asleep in their little wooden bed. In the distance, the cheery ringing of the bells of cows grazing in the mountain meadows invited them to get up. The two of them were just starting their vacation in Savoy, Switzerland, at the house of their cousins, the twins Theo and Leo. The children were soon on their feet and were visibly excited, because today was a big day. Their uncle, who was a mountain guide, was taking them to climb their first *via ferrata*, a protected climbing route up the mountain.

Breakfast was already ready, and a good smell had spread through the chalet. Questions rang out from all sides. Philomena spoke up first, because she was a little nervous. She lived in Paris and so she was not used to the mountains.

"Uncle William, is the via ferrata really hard to climb?"

"No, not at all, not at all," her uncle assured her. "Your cousins have already gone up them many times, and they just love it."

"There are iron bars fastened into the rock that are like steps. You only have to climb from one step to the next," young Theo explained. The two cousins had always gotten along well together.

"But it's dangerous, then," Philomena insisted, still rather nervous.

"No, nothing can happen to you," said Leo, the other twin. "My dad will put a harness on you. It's made of straps and fits over your clothes. It's really solid, and it will be attached to a rope so you can't fall."

Seeing her cousins' unshakable confidence, Philomena calmed down and got busy gulping down her breakfast so she would have plenty of strength, as her uncle had advised her. Finally, the little group of explorers was ready. All the equipment they needed was loaded into the car that was to take them on the expedition. They went on a beautiful road that climbed by zigzags and switchbacks up the side of the mountain. They stopped at the edge of a beautiful blue lake, Lac de la Rosière.

"Come on, I'll help you put on your climbing harnesses and helmets," said their guide.

"Why the helmets?" asked Philomena.

"Because stones might fall on your head, stones loosened by people climbing above you," replied the guide, very professionally.

Gaspard was not listening to any of this. He seemed to be worried about something. Very steep mountains rose on both sides of the beautiful blue lake, and Gaspard could already feel his knees beginning to wobble and shake.

"Can I go behind you, Uncle William?" Gaspard asked.

"If you like," his uncle replied in a reassuring tone, adjusting Gaspard's helmet. "We'll put Philomena between the twins, and I'll take care of you."

The happy group of climbers, all roped together, started off after their guide. The children took hold of the iron rungs one by one and climbed without a problem.

"In the end, it's not that complicated," Philomena thought. She was not finding it hard. But Gaspard kept looking down and seeing the lake becoming smaller and smaller beneath him. Next they had to cross a rope bridge called a monkey bridge. And then after that came the Nepali bridge over the lake, which swung from side to side a little as they walked over it.

They were continuing their climb uneventfully when suddenly a cry rang out. Uncle William was shouting: "Look out! Falling rock." But it came too late. The cry had come from Philomena, who had had a big stone fall on her helmet. This made a tremendous noise in her head, and partly from fear and partly from surprise, she completely let go of her handholds. Fortunately, as she was reassured to discover, the harness and the rope held her quite securely. But nevertheless, there she was, dangling in space about three feet below the rungs of the via ferrata, her skinny legs flailing in the air.

"Theo, switch your carabiners down to the rungs your feet are on now. Step out of the via ferrata and reach over and give your cousin your hand so she can climb back on," his father calmly told him.

"Okay, Dad, here I go," Theo replied.

But at this point Theo realized that there was a lot of empty space beneath him and his cousin was really pretty far away. He got kind of dizzy and didn't have the courage to leave the safety of the via ferrata and step directly onto the rock of the mountainside. Fear overcame him, and he was completely paralyzed.

"Help me, Yupsi!" Theo called out inside his head. For several months now, he had been friends with Yupsi the Little Dragon, and he knew that Yupsi was protecting him. Then suddenly he had no doubt. Yupsi would help Philomena for sure. With the dragon's tail as a staircase, she would easily be able to get back onto the iron rungs.

But to Theo's great surprise, this time, the little dragon did not appear. Theo only heard a little voice inside of him, which murmured,

"Theo, we have already done a lot of things together, and I know you have confidence in me. But starting today, you have to have confidence in yourself." Hearing these words, Theo suddenly had the feeling that the little dragon had slipped inside him. Yupsi continued to talk: "Since you want to do something good by helping Philomena, your heart will guide you, and you will succeed. Don't forget, Theo, I am with you. Use the magic breath."

Theo had confidence in Yupsi. He breathed out with all his might, imagining that the fear and dizziness were going out of him in a puff of black smoke. Then he felt full of inspiration and was able to store up all the energy and force that came into him in the form of white air when he breathed in. He repeated the breathing a few times until he felt the fear leave him. Then he unsnapped the first carabiner and snapped it onto the rung below, and he did the same with the second one. Next he put his foot on the rock that his father pointed out to him and reached out with his hand as far as he could and succeeded in grasping Philomena's hand. The little girl felt reassured at once and climbed with a leap across the rock and got back on the via ferrata. Theo, who was overjoyed, began yelling "Yippee! Yippee!" From the bottom of his heart, he thanked the little dragon for all the help and support he had given him.

The adventure was soon over and everybody settled down on the shore of the Lac de la Rosière for a well-deserved picnic. All that they had gone through had given the children a very good appetite. Raising his eyes to the electric blue sky, Theo saw a little cloud in the form of a little dragon, who seemed to be giving him a loving wink.

Just like Yupsi the Little Dragon
Open your eyes
Open your heart
You will see how good it is
To help others
That is happiness!

Now it's time for the three breaths! You can find the meditation on page 60 (for the little ones) and page 93 (for the older ones).

10 Meditations for Older Kids, Starting at Age Five

Now your child is ready to move past her first meditation with her teddy bear. This is the new routine for every evening:

- Open your heart to others (read of a tale on compassion)
- Sound (play the "Yupsi Song")
- Meditation on the Breath (White Light and Black Smoke, page 93)
- Meditation on Appreciation (appreciating your day, page 95)
- Gradual introduction of the Self-Reflection Meditation (page 29)

The routine is going to stay the same, but with slightly more elaborate meditations and a gradual introduction of the Self-Reflection Meditation. The form this meditation takes will depend a lot on your child's individual personality and his degree of maturity. It's up to you as a parent to gauge when the moment is right to extend your child's practice and to present this meditation in a way that works for him.

Meditation on the Breath: White Light and Black Smoke

Here you're going to do the exercise on the breath, the same one you did when you were younger, but a little more complete, because you have grown up more and you are now able to do it in almost the same way as your mom and dad.

Now take the posture that you know so well.

Begin by breathing out through both nostrils and thinking that everything nasty and bad goes out through your nose in a puff of black smoke. Are you really imagining the black smoke coming out of your nose?

1. Block your left nostril with the index finger of your left hand and breathe in deeply through your right nostril. Think of all the good things that can happen to you as entering your nose in the form of a white light. . . . Let your left hand rest in your lap and hold the air in your belly for one or two seconds.

2. Then with the index finger of your right hand, block your right nostril and exhale the air in the form of black smoke through your left nostril. . . . All the things that you don't like go away. . . . Pause briefly.

3. Keep your right nostril blocked and breathe in again through your left nostril. Think of all the good things that happen to

you as a beautiful white light that enters you through your nose. Rest your right hand in your lap and hold the air in your belly for a second.

4. Now block your left nostril with the index finger of your left hand and breathe everything that bothers you and seems wrong and bad out through your right nostril. Imagine that all that leaves you in the form of black smoke. Rest your left hand in your lap. . . . Pause briefly.

5. Through both nostrils, breathe in deeply all the good, positive thoughts, visualizing them as a white light that enters your body. . . . Hold the air in your belly for a second.

6. Exhale strongly through both nostrils to blow out all the bad, negative thoughts, visualizing them as black smoke going out your nose. . . . Pause briefly.

And there you are—you're all done! (It's a good idea to do this exercise three times. When you start a new series of breaths, start again by blocking your left nostril.)

Observe what you are feeling. Are you feeling better because the black smoke took away everything that was bothering you? Did the beautiful white light bring you a good feeling? If you got mixed up with the fingers and the nostrils, don't worry. That happens to all children in the beginning. But you'll learn fast, and the exercise will quickly become very natural. You also have to learn to find your own breathing rhythm. Very slow and relaxed. As you grow up, you will find this form of meditation very easy and you can do it anywhere. It will help you a lot to do well in school, on your exams, and even in your work later on.

Meditation on Appreciation

1. Sit down on your cushion as you usually do, or on the edge of your bed. Close your eyes, and think of everything good that has happened to you during the day today.

2. Think of your teacher and all the nice things she did for you. . . . Think of all the good things that happened at school. . . . Think of your parents and everything they did for you. . . . Think of the good times you had with your friends. . . .

3. Now you can also reach out with your thoughts to your grandparents, to your brothers and sisters (if your child has any), to your godfather and your godmother (if your child has them), your uncles and aunts, your cousins, and your whole family. Did they do anything nice for you today? . . . No doubt they all love you a lot. Appreciate that.

4. Appreciate also that you are in good health (if that is the case). Appreciate not being sick.

5. Appreciate having nice friends who you can have fun with. Think of all the children in the world.

6. Stay silent if you can for at least a minute in order to appreciate all that.

7. *Observe what you are feeling.* Are you feeling full of love and joy? Are you feeling really happy?

Dedication to All the Children in the World

Now Yupsi is doing a dedication. He is sending loving wishes for you and all the children in the whole world. Do as Yupsi is doing. Wish from the bottom of your heart for all children to be happy. You can say these words out loud: "I wish all the children in the world not to suffer, not to be sick, and to be happy always!"

Good night!

Walking Meditation

If you would like to loosen up your legs, Yupsi knows another meditative exercise that's very simple and fun. It's one of his favorite exercises. You can train in walking meditation—at home, in the park, with your friends on the playground, or even on the street. The best thing is to take advantage of a quiet place like the seaside or the mountains if you ever have a chance to visit those places, or if you live there.

Make the most of each step.

1. In a standing position, stay still for a few seconds. Breathe gently into your belly (remember the movement of your little

teddy bear when it moved back and forth with your breath). Your feet feel heavy and rest firmly on the floor. Have your arms in front of you, relaxed, then put the back of your left hand just below your navel, palm up. Then cover the palm of your left hand with the palm of your right hand. Close your hands one over the other, without tensing up.

2. Gaze at a point in front of you. Feel or imagine the breeze coming off the sea and caressing your face, or just feel nature around you.

3. Now begin to walk. Lift your right heel, breathe in, swelling your belly (remember your teddy bear moving forward). Raise your right foot and move your leg slowly forward. Feel your breath rising up toward your lungs and feel your rib cage swelling. Let your thoughts come and go, but don't get into a big conversation with yourself.

4. Put your right foot down and breathe out as you place it on the floor. In breathing out, push upward with your belly. Your belly will hollow out (remember your teddy bear moving back in). Then your rib cage will contract. Press your foot firmly on the floor. Appreciate the ground under your foot. Let your thoughts come and go.

5. Now lift your left heel and inhale deeply, filling your belly. Lift your left foot and move your leg slowly forward. Feel your breath moving up toward your lungs and your rib cage swelling. Let your thoughts come and go.

6. Put your left foot down and breathe out as you do so. As you breathe out, push your belly upward. Your belly hollows out

and your rib cage contracts. Take your time. Appreciate the ground under your foot.

Go ahead and repeat this for a few minutes, one foot after the other.

In walking meditation, it is important to observe your breathing. If you're not sure you're doing the breathing right, Yupsi has a tip for you. During the first two or three breaths, in order to check up on the movement of your lungs as well as the movement of your belly, put your hands against your body on each side of your waist. Check first to make sure that your belly is swelling and contracting, and then check that your lungs are swelling and contracting. Learning to breathe properly is important for your health. You can also check up on your breathing during your everyday life. Think of blowing out your birthday candles or blowing the fuzz off a dandelion while pushing with your belly.

Observe all your emotions. Use the slow rhythm of your steps and breathing to calm yourself, little by little. Stay connected to your surroundings. This is a very fine way to have a very good day.

You don't necessarily have to do walking meditation all by yourself. You can also do it with friends—single file, one behind the other. But watch out now—remember to keep up your concentration and stay silent.

The Gift Stickers Test: Your Child's Level of Compassion after Ten Weeks of the Program

Yupsi has once again brought you a whole lot of gifts. But who are you going to give them to this time? (Give the sheet of stickers to your child.) You can give them to your best friend, to a child you don't know, to a child who is sick or has had an accident, or to somebody in your class who you always find annoying.

Now stick the stickers on the gift boxes. You can give as many as you want to whomever you want.

What has changed since the first test?

Your best friend

Total

Unknown child

Total

Sick child

Total

The child who annoys you the most

Total

Conclusion

A Lifelong Project for Your Child

You as a parent will most likely want to join your child in the adventure of meditation. You now know that the results are really worth the effort, and you have found a new sense of closeness and togetherness with your child from doing the meditation exercises together.

Thanks to Yupsi's magic breath, your child will gradually develop a solid psychological balance that will help her deal with the difficulties of the contemporary world. It is also possible that your child is already calmer, less inclined to get angry, and sleeping better. This would be very encouraging, but it's essential that your child continue to practice in order to maintain these results. By training the mind in altruism and self-concentration, your child will develop a different relationship with others, become compassionate, and have more respect for animals and the environment.

Let us hope that this enlightened form of education will catch on and spread so that a new generation of children will create a society in which everyone can live with less stress and more joy. This goal is not out of reach—and your child and your family have already begun to realize it, with the help of Yupsi the Little Dragon.

Acknowledgments

We would like to thank all those who offered us their support on this project.

Our greatest gratitude goes to our spiritual masters. Without the constant support of their wisdom and compassion, we would not have been able to write this book: His Holiness the Gyalwang Drukpa, spiritual head of the Drukpa lineage—*druk* means "dragon"—one of the main Buddhist schools of the Himalayan region, founded by the great Indian saint Naropa, whose thousandth birthday was celebrated in Ladakh, northern India, in July 2016. And His Eminence Gyalwa Dokhampa, Jigme Pema Nyinjadh, recognized by the Dalai Lama as the ninth incarnation of the Gyalwa Dokhampa, who was enthroned in Bhutan, a country where the Drukpa lineage teachings are the religion of the state. His teachings, youthful, dynamic, and particularly accessible for beginners like us, have been a great source of inspiration.

We thank our friends Agnès Vidalie and Amélie Poggi from Éditions Marabout for having thought of asking us to add to our book a section dedicated to parents. We also thank Hélène Gédouin, the editorial director, who supported our project.

Acknowledgments

We thank our friends who had the patience to read through the text of this book several times: Jeanne Bouchet, who made big improvements, Cécile Servais, for the quality and richness of her comments, and Danièle Bonnevie, for sharing with us his knowledge of the world of animals, which was very helpful for our tales.

Thanks to Guillaume Prin for composing our lovely "Yupsi Song."

Thanks to Olivier Adam for her unfailing support and contagious enthusiasm.

Thanks to Mario Salort of Éditions Marabout, who understood our project so well and who provided us with the support needed to finalize it; to Lucie Léna, who so kindly guided us in the world of publishing, which was unknown to us; to Adejie, to whom we owe so many beautiful illustrations.

And very special thanks to Matthieu Ricard for his subtle understanding of our project and for the profundity of his foreword.

"The Child from Ladakh" continues past the final page of the story. Young Tsering Dorje enrolled in the Druk Padma Karpo School in Shey, Ladakh, Northern India. The school is a pilot project with an ecological emphasis that has more than a thousand pupils. If you would like to add your support to that of the authors and thus help make it possible for other young children to go to school, you can contact the school directly at www.dwls.org/druk-padma-karpo-school-/-druk-white-lotus-school-shey-ladakh.html or at the foundation Live to Love France (www.livetolove.org), which sponsors this school and runs a number of humanitarian projects in India, Bhutan, and Nepal (where it is very active in the reconstruction of the country).

Notes

CHAPTER 2: Why Meditate?

1. Daniel Goleman, *Social Intelligence: The New Science of Human Relationships* (New York: Bantam Books, 2007), 12.
2. Ibid., 13.
3. Christophe André, et al., *Se changer, changer le monde* (Paris: L'Iconoclaste, 2013).
4. Goleman, *Social Intelligence*, 319.

CHAPTER 3: Which Meditation Practice to Choose?

1. Matthieu Ricard, *Why Meditate? Working with Thoughts and Emotions* (Carlsbad, CA: Hay House, 2010), 49–50. Slightly edited.
2. Gyalwa Dokhampa, *The Restful Mind* (Hodder & Stoughton, Kindle edition, 2013).
3. Op. cit., Kindle locations 968–75.

CHAPTER 6: Introduction to the Yupsi Method

1. Ricard Matthieu, *Plaidoyer pour l'altruisme* (Nil Éditions, 2014), 608–25.